DESTINATION ADULTHOOD

Thanks for your support!
Graham

First published in Great Britain in 2019

Copyright © 2019 by Graham Sykes

All rights reserved

No part of this book may be reproduced or used in any manner without written permission of the copyright owner except for the use of quotations in a book review.

Although the author and publisher have made every effort to ensure that the information in this book was correct at the time of print, the author and publisher do not assume and hereby disclaim any liability to any party for any loss, damage, or disruption caused by errors or omissions, whether such errors or omissions result from negligence, accident, or any other cause.

This book is not intended as a substitute for the medical advice of doctors and GPs. The reader should regularly consult a doctor in matters relating to their physical & mental health and particularly with respect to any symptoms that may require diagnosis or medical attention.

First paperback edition September 2019

Book design by Fourteen19®

ISBN 978-1-9133-1903-8 (Paperback)

www.destination.org.uk

This book is dedicated to everyone who has supported my journey from a 16 year old who left school without a GCSE in English, to someone who now advises national organisations and government on communicating with teens and young adults.

I'd like to thank the thousands of young people who have taken part in conversations, undertaken surveys or participated in focus groups over the years; and to everyone who has helped with the journey of writing this book. Those who guided its direction and provided insight and feedback at the various stages of its development.

Particular thanks go to Susan for the red thread and Lucy P, Lucy H, and Amy B for giving up their time to read early drafts. A special thanks also goes out to Dave P and the students at Brooksbank Sixth Form College who continue to provide an invaluable resource to myself and my clients.

Finally, as is customary on these occasions I'd like to thank Kate (for proofing it *twice*), S&V, my family and friends and all my current, previous & future clients.

I really couldn't have done any of this without you.

Contents

Part One: Getting ready for the journey ahead   9
Introduction, Preparing For The Journey Ahead
Free Gift

Part Two: Do you need a reset?   24
Do You Need A 'Reset'?

Part Three: The 12 LifeLocations® you need to consider   32

1:	Education	36
2:	Employment	56
3.	Life Skills	89
4:	Networks	101
5:	Money	107
6:	Health & Wellbeing	129
7:	Housing	145
8:	Where You Live	158
9:	Family & Friends	167
10:	Community & Democracy	172
11:	Transport	184
12:	Travelling	200

Extra Section: This All Sounds Too Much, Why Don't I Just Become A Rich, Famous Celebrity!   **213**

Part Four: Making it work for you   222
Reset, Plan, Take Responsibility &
Make It Happen

Part One: Getting ready for the journey ahead

Before Beyoncé, before Apple and long before YouTube lived a man called Aristotle. He was born in Ancient Greece in 384BC - which is about 2,400 years ago.

> *Look, don't worry if this sounds a bit off-topic and daunting - it's trying to demonstrate how something potentially off-putting can be made simple and understandable.*
>
> *You'll find this throughout the book - things that you might think at first aren't for you, but on further thought are actually quite understandable.*
>
> *Anyway, where were we? Oh yes Ancient Greece...*

Aristotle was a philosopher and he developed many theories that are still acknowledged today. One of his best known is that "the whole is greater than the sum of its parts."

What this means is that when you bring a number of elements together, they are more effective than they would have been on their own. It's like the concept of teamwork - when people work together they often create more than they would have done individually.

It also happens to be the basic premise of the Infinity Stones in the Avengers films. On their own they are powerful but when you bring them all together you can rule the world - possibly (Spoiler Alert)!

I believe that everyone's journey to Destination Adulthood involves visiting twelve LifeLocations®.

The twelve LifeLocations® are:

1: Education
2: Employment
3: Life Skills
4: Networks
5: Money
6: Health & Wellbeing
7: Housing
8: Where you live
9: Family & Friends
10: Community & Democracy
11: Transport
12: Travelling

Whilst individually each of these LifeLocations® will play an important role in how your journey to adulthood progresses, you need to harness them collectively. This will ensure you reach your Destination Adulthood and maximise the potential that you have as a young adult.

Pre-adulthood you have a choice: You can choose to take control of each LifeLocation® and mould it into the life you want to have, or you can let the locations shape themselves and let fate be in charge of your destiny.

In order to secure what you want from life as an adult, you will need to build a picture of what you want your ideal Destination Adulthood to look like. Only then can you consider what you need from each location along the journey to make it happen. Like Aristotle said: 'the whole is greater than the sum of its parts'. Individually, each LifeLocation® will be unable to provide you with your ideal adult life, but when you address them all and bring them together as a whole, your Destination Adulthood will be much nearer to achieving.

Everyone's 'Destination Adulthood' is different. Some people will chase money and success, some will want security, some will just want to be happy and some will be driven to make a difference to the lives of people around them. We are all different, but the LifeLocations® that define adulthood are not. It is just that in order to create your specific Destination Adulthood, some locations will be more important to define than others.

Whether or not you reach your Destination Adulthood will ultimately depend on the preparation and effort that you put into each of the LifeLocations® along your journey.

As you get older, one of the first lessons you will learn as an adult is that nobody gives you anything easily. This will be made worse by the fact that when you look around, you will feel that other people (particularly those that you don't know and who are from other backgrounds) seem to have it much easier. They will be the people who look as though they are getting all the opportunities, all the breaks, and all the benefits at your expense. In truth, this is probably half correct. Some people will be in a more fortunate position that you, but there will also be people in a worse position - people who are looking at you and thinking you have it easy!

You might make yourself feel better by feeling sorry for yourself and blaming your lack of opportunities on others, but where is this going to get you? Surrounding yourself with negativity is a guaranteed way of not reaching your ideal Destination Adulthood. This is not going to be an easy journey. It is going to be tough and it is going to require you to make sacrifices and in some cases possibly change the direction of your life.

For something this important, you are going to have to try to put 100% effort into everything you do. If you don't, and someone else does (and as a result gets the opportunity that *you* wanted) then you have to expect to lose out to them and you only have yourself to blame. Effort is not defined by someone's background, their parents, or their previous opportunities, it is defined by determination.

Life isn't always fair, so you will need to find a way to get over it. The good news is that you are already addressing it by reading this book. Within these pages is all the help you need to identify the opportunities that you should be taking advantage of. It will provide you with a guide to help you reach your Destination Adulthood in the most successful way possible. Whether you already have a clearly identified path or have no idea of the journey you are about to make – this book will show you how to get the most from each individual location and help you to reach your Destination Adulthood.

Preparing for the journey ahead: How to use this book

Who reads books anymore? Actually quite a few people do. Physical books have many advantages that e-books and apps don't have. The main one being that a book provides you with quick access to a guide that will be invaluable as you proceed on your journey towards your Destination Adulthood.

The route ahead is never straight forward and will be filled with many twists and turns. It is therefore important that you have constant access to a trusted information source that you can either read in its entirety or dip in and out of when you need it.

By keeping it on a shelf or in a drawer, you will know that it is always available to provide advice when you need it. As it is your book you can do what you want with it. You can make notes within it, you can lend it to friends, or you can use it to prop up a wobbly table – it's completely up to you. It has been written in a way that the content should be relevant to any person who wants to reach their own Destination Adulthood.

In Part Three you will find the twelve individual LifeLocations®

that you need to consider in your overall journey to create and reach your Destination Adulthood. These include key sections about making sure you have basic qualifications, about getting a job, having enough money and putting a roof over your head through to less critical (but equally important) issues such as having your own transport, broadening your horizons via travelling and how to vote in elections.

Sometimes before we can go forward we need to take a step or two backwards. In Part Two we discuss how sometimes it is necessary to reset aspects our lives so that we can overcome potential issues that are holding us back. Resetting allows us to be able to advance successfully to the next stage of the journey. After each chapter we will look at a number of examples of potential resets that you might want to consider in order to maximise the opportunities available to you.

About me

Don't worry, this book is not about trying to make you grow up. This period of time between being a teenager and an adult should be one of the best times in your life. You will never have more time, more freedom and more opportunities to shape your life, than you do now.

But that doesn't mean that you should put your headphones on (or in) and ignore some of the difficult decisions that are starting to appear on the horizon.

For the last twenty-five years I've been working with teens and young adults to make them aware of the thousands of opportunities that are available to help them improve their lives on a daily, monthly and yearly basis. I do this by helping organisations with beneficial products & services present themselves in a way that people will notice them and think "that sounds interesting – let me find out more". Over this time, I have become one of the UK's leading experts in helping bring brands, organisations and young adults together.

I wanted to put all the experience that I have accumulated into one helpful guide that will help individuals navigate from being a teen to an adult.

This book is the culmination of thousands of hours of conversations with 16 to 24 year olds from around the country on a wide range of subjects. Not only do I run a successful youth marketing consultancy, but I have also helped advise the Government, and have actively mentored a number of young adults who have gone on to take advantages of opportunities and develop successful careers that wouldn't have normally been available to them.

I could have written this guide in a jokey style, but most of the people I have spoken to said that something this important should be produced in a serious way. Hopefully you will find the spirit that I have written it in is still fun & interesting, and that you will ultimately benefit from the hints, tips and advice contained within it.

Within this book I have tried to format it in a way that will be easy to understand and allow you to either dip in and out of it when you need to, or binge-read it like a Netflix boxset.

> *If you need any further convincing – I left school at 16 with 4 GCSE's (of which English wasn't one of them). I re-sat it at sixth-form college alongside three A Levels that I managed to get minimal passes in. I got a job in a building society and worked there for three years until I decided to make the big decision to leave and go to university.*
>
> *With a 2:1 in Business Studies and Public Media, I set up a marketing company and for more years than I can remember I have worked hard trying to keep it successful. I'm from a modest background and certainly have never been given any life changing opportunities in my life. I learnt early that if you want something, you cannot rely on others to do it for you.*

And now I have written a book. If I'd told myself at 16 (having just failed my English GCSE) that it would even be possible - let alone by me – I'd have laughed in their face. Which all goes to show, anything is possible. It's just up to you to make it happen.

When do we become an adult?

Whilst legally we all become an adult at the age of 18, the actual point we 'grow up' and reach the destination of adulthood is different for everyone. No one wants to become an adult, but the day you realise that you have reached Destination Adulthood is the day that your journey has ended. Prior to your arrival you have a variety of routes available, but once you become an adult (and have acquired all the responsibilities and commitments that go along with it), it's very difficult to plot a different outcome.

Whether you had a rough, an okay or a great time going through school, this is no guarantee that everything will continue to follow the same path. In the first part of your life there were a number of people looking out for you (teachers, parents, extended family and friends, social workers, or in some cases maybe the local newsagent) even if you didn't realise it.

This means that up to the age of 18, you have been massively supported. You might not have realised it, but every photocopied handout, every reminder to attend a session, every person or company they brought in to talk to you was designed to make you the best possible version of yourself. However, at 18 (or whenever you leave school or college) that stops like a bullet. From now on – you are largely on your own.

Fortunately, this book is going to help you.

What is expected from you?

All that is asked is that you give up a few hours of your life to read this book and think about how the twelve LifeLocations® could affect you. If you do this, I believe that you will reap the benefits for many years to come. My aim is that by reading it, you will be more equipped to deal with the adult-stuff that no one ever tells you that you need know about.

Throughout this book you will also find numerous suggestions of things that you should do and/or take advantage of. But ultimately, whether you do or not will be up to you. The main advantage that you have as a young person is time. Whilst you may be financially poor, you are certainly time rich. You might not realise it now, but in years to come you will look back in disbelief at the amount of free time you had.

Even by reading a few pages, or adopting a few of the suggestions – you'll be better off.

I have written and developed this book with a team of young assistants. Every word I have written has been scrutinised by them to ensure that it is understandable by a wide cross-section of people and relevant to a teen/young adult age group. If they weren't happy with a word or a section – it has been removed. This means that everything you read has been 'youth approved' by a team of teens and young adults just like you.

One of their suggestions was that the book should include some space and tables for you to jot down your thoughts as you read. The last thing I want is for this to become a workbook – but if you find it useful to record your ideas then please go for it. It is your book after all.

Destination Adulthood is underpinned by four key principles that will be repeated constantly through all the chapters. We will explain these in more details as we progress – but in summary they are:
1) Nobody's final destination is pre-determined and everyone has the opportunity to press the reset button on their life choices at any time
2) Everyone's destination is different
3) In order to reach your destination, you need a plan
4) It is your responsibility to make sure you reach it

Work out what is important in life

If you take one thing from reading Destination Adulthood, it's that you don't need to have everything as a teen or young adult. I've worked in advertising – and I understand that some brands and organisations will do anything they can to sell you the dream that your life is incomplete without product X or brand Y. Once you accept that having everything you want is just a cynical advertising ploy – you can actually look at accumulating the things that you need now and that are actually going to benefit you.

A famous and clever academic called Maslow wrote a theory called the 'Hierarchy of Needs'. Within it he states that 'shelter' and 'food' are a person's main priorities and it is essential to have these before you move onto the things that are less important but are nice to have.

Now we have all blown our first wage or student loan payment on something decadent and stupid – *Why not, it's a rite of passage!* - but you can only keep on doing this if you know that another payment is coming along shortly.

On average most people live until they are about 80; which if you are 18, means you have 62 years ahead of you. Life is a journey, and as you progress you will hopefully accumulate more (and better) things. Having the latest phone is great, but if you are going to spend more on it than you do on food, or putting a roof over your head – then you have some priorities that are wrong somewhere along the line.

Putting a few luxuries on hold now, will mean you will be able to afford them in a few years time and much, much more. Demanding and accumulating everything now will ultimately just hold you back for many years to come.

Helping you answer the most important question in the world

There is a question that everybody asks every day and it dictates and underpins every decision you will ever make:

What's in it for me?

You might not always be aware of it – but whenever an opportunity is presented to you, a little sub-conscious voice in your head will ask: "What's in it for me?"

This isn't a voice that is exclusive to young people. Whether you are 18 or 80, people invariably only do something if they want to (or if they can see a benefit at the end of it). The problem when you are 18 is that you don't always have the experience or knowledge to know what the benefit is going to be. Sure – people will tell you it is in your interest, but ultimately you need to see it to make the decision yourself.

Destination Adulthood will help you to see the journey ahead and give you an idea of some of the things that you will have to deal with as an adult. Once you are aware of the twists and turns of being a grown up, you will become aware of the help you are going to need. This will then make you more receptive to the opportunities that are going to help you reach your Destination Adulthood when they are presented to you.

But remember, everybody is different and everyone who reads this book will take something different from it.

This is now your book and you can do what you want with it. Whether it becomes an essential guide to life or simply a way of hiding things in plain sight (see opposite) – I hope you find it useful for many years to come.

Your Free Gift

Well done for making it this far!

If you have been bought this book and you don't fancy reading it anymore then you have three choices:

1) Read it anyway – you might find it useful
2) Flip the pages a bit, bend the front cover and put it on a shelf so that the person who bought it you thinks you have read it or
3) Use the guide below to turn this book into a place to hide secret things

To turn this book into a place to hide all (or some of) your secret things simply cut out the shape within the dotted line and repeat for the next hundred pages. You will then create a space to hide secret things.

By the way, if you can be bothered to do this – you can definitely be bothered to read this book. And you won't risk cutting your fingers off and hurting yourself.

Still ready for Destination Adulthood? Let's get on with it…

Part Two:
Do you need a 'reset'?

Everyone has travelled a different path in the first stage of their life and it is human nature to think that everyone else is in a more fortunate position that you. Looking at other people you might think they are more qualified than you, from a better background, cleverer, richer, luckier, better looking, and/or more confident – but the reality is that they probably aren't. If they are – so what? That was in the past, from now on we are focused on looking forward!

Everything you have done in your life so far has led to the current version of you – but it doesn't have to define the rest of your life. You may have found that navigating the first part of your life was difficult. Some people realise that school didn't suit them, some people have to deal with challenging home lives, and some people get in with the wrong crowd; but there is no reason why you have pay for your childhood experiences for the rest of your life.

We all need a reset from time to time. Sometimes it's just a case of giving ourselves a kick up the bum, but for other times it's about fundamentally changing our direction in life – and admittedly this can seem daunting and difficult.

This is why we are all a little bit like technology – sometimes we need a 'soft reset' and every now again, a 'factory reset'.

Like a phone, if it isn't working properly you can't just expect to give it a shake and expect it to start functioning without giving it a bit of attention. Whilst switching it 'off and back on' might solve some issues, sometimes you have to take more serious measures. Sometimes this might involve having to go and get expert help to put it right.

The reality is that to make the most of your life, you may need to consider some form of reset from time to time. If something is holding you back and preventing you from reaching your Destination Adulthood, you need to put it right and overcome it.

It is very likely that you don't even know some of the reasons that are holding you back. Within each LifeLocation® you will see the skills and knowledge that you are going to need to succeed. Still no idea of what job you want to do? - *that is going to hold you back*. Don't have a maths or English GCSE? - *that is going to hold you back too*.

Each location will also show you the things that you need to know and the areas that you need to be thinking about. *Again, don't worry.* This is not something you need to sort in the next few hours, it's about planting a seed in your mind and letting it slowly grow so that when the time comes, you are ready to deal with the issues that come with getting older.

Treat today as 'Day One'

Wherever you feel you rank in relation to other young adults – it doesn't matter, because by treating today as 'Day One', and by resetting the areas that are holding you back, you will soon be equal with everyone else.

What you achieve from now on will be down to you. Sure, some people might still have it easier than you, but all that means is that you are going to have to work a bit harder (and smarter) to catch them up.

> *Here are two pieces of inside knowledge:*
> *1) This book is going to help you level up with everyone else, and,*
> *2) Remember, even though they might not show it – everyone thinks that somebody else has it better than they do!*

History is littered with stories of people who have gone from rags to riches or overcome major adversities to get what they want. If you want it bad enough – you can get it. And if you are still reading – you are well on your way to reaching a successful Destination Adulthood.

Why not use the table at the end of this section to record the areas of your life that could benefit from a reset. Obviously, this might be personal, and you might not want to document it in a book – and that's fine. If you want to keep your thoughts private perhaps you could record it in the notes section of your phone? It might be that you don't even know the things that need resetting yet. This is why you might want to keep coming back to this as we progress throughout the book. Let's face it – performing a number of small resets is much easier than undertaking one big one.

As we start to look at the various LifeLocations® that you need to consider on your journey to your Destination Adulthood, you will be able to decide which areas of your life need resetting. For example, you might not have English or maths GCSEs, but by resetting that and going back to college and studying hard to get them – this will make a massive difference to your life. Almost immediately you will find that there are more job vacancies available to apply for and that they have a higher starting salary. Likewise, if you lack confidence or communication skills resetting this part of yourself and pushing yourself out of your comfort zone might result in you overcoming other challenges.

The LifeLocations® I've identified are the areas that I think are the most important – and the areas I think you need to know about.

At some point in the coming years you are going to need to get a job, find somewhere to live and manage your money. As part of this you are going to need to build networks, understand how the country works, and help yourself by being physically & mentally healthy. Being an adult is tough but it's important you arrive at your Destination Adulthood fresh and ready to enjoy it.

The 'Soft reset'

There is nothing wrong with feeling as though you are in a good place. There is nothing to be embarrassed about if you have good exam results, are/were good at school and are generally happy with your life.

However, having spoken to lots of teens and young adults as part of my job, it would appear that most people have some nagging doubts in their mind about something they are unhappy with.

The last thing you want is for the negative part of you to hold you back.

As you progress you will be able to consider what skills, qualities and knowledge you need in order to maximise your potential. From here you will then be able to calculate what action you need to take to put them right. It might be nothing more than putting together a small plan or watching a few informational YouTube videos.

You will be amazed at the difference it will make even by making a few small resets.

The 'Factory reset'

Okay, let's face it some of us depart our younger years not in a great place. But this doesn't mean that we have to carry it around with us like a badge of dishonour for the rest of time. Through no fault of your own (or even if it is your fault), you might be in a bad way and in need of a major reset in your life.

It can feel as though changing direction is an impossible task and one that you don't have the skills or energy to tackle. You might feel as though some personal issues can't be overcome, but as we proceed, you are going to discover that there are some things that you are good at and some that you are less good at. Hopefully by understanding this you will be able to undertake a more involved reset.

No one is expecting you to do everything on your own. As you will discover, there are lots of people and organisations that purely exist to help people reach their Destination Adulthood successfully.

There are thousands of opportunities 'out there' that you could take advantage of, that will be beneficial as you advance into adulthood.

Don't be alarmed if you haven't noticed them – lots of organisations who offer life-benefitting products and services to young people aren't very good at promoting their services. They advertise in places that young adults don't frequent and they use imagery and language that puts people off. These organisations are great at employing professionals who can help young adults reset aspects of their lives – but if they aren't great at promoting them (or cannot afford to do it properly), fewer young people take up their services.

It will be a constant theme of this book that you have to take the responsibility to search out and engage with the products and services that are going to enable you to reach your Destination Adulthood.

Take careers advice for example. Each town or city will have an organisation that is responsible for helping young people explore careers opportunities. Just because they haven't knocked on your door and offered you a chauffeur-driven limousine to attend one of their meetings isn't necessarily their fault. Quite often the onus will be on you to search out the support that you have identified that you need.

To use the technology comparisons again, sometimes your phone or computer just won't work without it being looked at by an expert – and sometimes, when it can't be fixed in store it is sent away for a different expert to look at it. If you feel that your problems can't be fixed, maybe it's because there isn't just one solution and that its going to take a number of experts to help you. And like your phone or computer it isn't going to be sorted in one day.

Until you start the reset process you don't know what is going to be involved and how long it is going to take. If you need to take the 'factory reset' option to prepare you for adulthood then it is going to take time – but 'time' is something that you have lots of when you are younger.

The hardest part of the process is knowing where to start – and this is something we are going to discuss a lot. We will discuss the people and organisations that can help you to take lots of small steps on a longer journey. Once you have a plan - you will be well on your way.

Look out for the reset buttons at the end of each section and consider whether you need to reset your journey for any of the destinations discussed.

Areas that require a reset:	Soft Reset	Factory Reset
Education		
Employment		
Life Skills		
Networks		
Money		
Health & Wellbeing		
Housing		
Family & Friends		
Where you live		
Community & Democracy		
Transport		
Travelling		

Part Three:
The 12 LifeLocations® you need to consider

Okay, it's time to get serious. Over the next twelve sections we are going to discuss the key LifeLocations® on the journey you are about to undertake. This will allow you to plan a route to maximise your potential, reach your Destination Adulthood and ensure that by the time you realise you are an adult – you will be in the best possible position to enjoy it for all its worth.

As we have said – when you become an adult you accrue lots of responsibilities – many of which you will be ill-prepared to deal with. However, by being aware of their existence and having access to a guide to deal with them, you will be two steps nearer to taking them in your stride.

But first you need to start making some decisions.

Everyone has a different idealised version of their Destination Adulthood. Some will want it all - the big house, the fast car, the family, the holidays and the designer clothes – whilst others will be happy irrespective of material goods. Everyone is different and therefore everyone will take a different route to get to their individual goal.

Knowing what you want to do when you grow up is a very difficult question to answer, and visualising the future is a very big concept to understand. It is a question however that you need to start thinking about. If you don't then it will be like starting a car journey without a 'sat-nav' or a map. Getting lost along the way is only going to take you longer to get there and cost you more money in fuel. Planning the route before you set off is much easier and beneficial in the long run.

To start your brain thinking, why not start by looking at the lives of your parents or your friend's parents and see if they have a lifestyle that you would like to emulate? If they do, what are the aspects that you like? Likewise, if they don't, why not?

One thing to consider though is this: Don't compare your current life to your parents or anybody else's parents. They started the journey to their Destination Adulthood years ago. They didn't simply acquire their lifestyle overnight – they have followed a route that has led them to this point. Remember you can only see the aspects of people's lifestyles that they make visible. Behind the curtains we are all dealing with our own unique problems.

Making some decisions at the start about what *your* unique Destination Adulthood looks like will enable you to formulate a plan on how to reach it. But don't forget, we are not carving this plan into stone. There is nothing to say that you can't change your mind and pursue a different destination at a later date. It's your life and you can reset it at any time you wish.

The only caveat (or warning) to this is that the older you get, the harder it is to change your life direction. It is very difficult when you have a job, a house and friends all based in a certain area to suddenly decide that you want to work and live at the other side of the country. Yes, it is do-able, but turning your back on an established life is really hard to do. It's much easier to try and work out now what you want and build your life choices around making it happen.

So keep asking yourself the same question: 'What do I want to do when I grow up?' The more detail you can provide, the more planning you can start to do to make it happen.

Within each of the following LifeLocations® a number of additional questions will be posed. These questions are designed to make you think about the subject and whether or not you are equipped with the skills and knowledge to advance this part of the journey to your Destination Adulthood. These questions are not designed to trick you or make you feel daft – they are there to help you realise what you don't know. None of us know what we don't know – but fortunately for you, some of these answers can be found in the pages of this book.

What do you want to do when you grow up?

LifeLocation®
1. Education

Unless you specifically sat your 11+ exams, or attended a private fee-paying school, it is unlikely that you chose your secondary school. Prior to the age of 16, your education was based on where you lived or where your parents chose to put you.

For many, reaching the age of 16 presents the first major decisions of your life. Do you study A Levels? Should you do a BTEC? Or do you say goodbye to full-time education and get a job or an Apprenticeship?

Whilst this can seem like a big decision, for many it isn't. By the age of 16, people tend to know if they have had enough of education or if they are going to continue and whether they want academic qualifications (A Levels) or something more practical (BTECs). It used to be that in order to go to university you had to go down the A Level route, but nowadays with many practical-based degrees, it is now possible to go to university with vocational-based qualifications such as BTECs or T Levels (from 2020).

It is important to know that there is no right or wrong

decision. Whichever you feel is right at the time is correct. The beauty of making a decision, is that if you want to, you can always change it at a later date. So even if you decide to take an Apprenticeship and it turns out to be the worse decision you've ever made – you can simply leave and either apply for another Apprenticeship or apply to college at the next available intake. Yes, you might be a year behind some of your mates but within the scheme of life it won't matter one bit. Remember, everyone's journey to adulthood is different and this includes how long it takes to get there.

Once you hit 16 you will find that everyone's career and education path starts to vary. Some will start courses at college, some will have to re-sit a year, some will start working, some will start work and then leave to go to college, and some will leave college and start working.

This is what is meant by resetting your life - no decision is set in stone. Maybe your exam results were better than expected which shows that you are more academic than you give yourself credit for. This could suggest that you could do more advanced qualifications or try and change your choice of sixth form college. Likewise, if your results were worse than expected, rather than give up you might want to re-enrol and re-sit them.

Remember it is the decisions that you make now that will start to effect your final Destination Adulthood. Even if you feel that they involve a step backwards now, you will notice that you jump two steps forward later on.
At 16, you face the first difficult decisions of your life but

whichever choice you make you will find that unexpected benefits come from it. For example, all these multiple pathways mean that you will come into contact with lots of new and different people which will result in your creating new friendship groups. All of a sudden that potentially 'wasted year' or difficult decision has introduced you to a whole new group of people who you could end up being friends with for the rest of your life.

Q. Should I go to sixth-form college?

What should you be looking for?

In your final year of secondary school (Year 11) you will be invited to attend Open Days hosted by sixth-form colleges hoping to convince you to apply to them.

Once again, there is responsibility on yourself to think about what you want to do.

Some, i.e. those who have their career mapped out, will probably not only know the college that they are going to attend, but the courses they are going to study. However, it is still worth visiting a number of different colleges just to get a feel for the variety of options available and to either reinforce your decision or change your mind.

For those that are unsure about what to do – don't worry – lots of people are in a similar situation. The key to making a decision is to choose subjects that you are interested in, that you enjoy, and are reasonably okay at.

Lots of people will try to give you advice – "do maths", "do English", "do a science", but the reality is that unless you want to study a specific subject at university (one that requires pre-defined A Levels), you are better off studying subjects you enjoy. You should also avoid choosing a college because your best friend(s) are going there. Again, if it's not for you – you will soon realise it.

At some point it is going to get tough and if you don't like the subject(s) you are studying, your enthusiasm will quickly diminish. If you start thinking "I wish I hadn't taken this subject – I only did it because [insert name of person here] said it would be a good idea – then you will soon find that you aren't doing as much work as you need to and that you are slipping behind.

Some inside information that you should know:

1. *Most universities (and Apprenticeships) aren't really bothered what subjects you have studied – they are more interested in the grades. If your university course gives you an offer of 'BBC'. (i.e. you need three A Levels with the grades B, B and C), it's going to be easier to get that in subjects that you enjoy, rather than ones that you don't (or find too hard).*
2. *If you are unsure what you want to do at university or as a career, then it makes sense that you are more likely to want a job in a subject that you are interested*

in. Studying subjects that you enjoy might be the first step to discovering a career that you didn't know existed.

Underpinning all your studies will be a good use of English & maths. If you didn't pass them at GCSE – then you will need to re-sit them at sixth-form college. Some colleges will insist that you pass them before starting A Levels, however, (if you have good passes in other subjects), most will let you start your A Levels and allow you to re-sit the qualification in Year 12, which will give you lots of time in year 13 to concentrate solely on your A Levels.

Q. What different types of colleges are there?

There are three types of college that you can attend after leaving school at 16:
1) A school sixth form
2) A stand-alone sixth form
3) A Further Education college

1) A school sixth-form

A school sixth-form will be attached to a school and in the main it will share the building or campus with students doing GCSEs. This can have both positives and negatives. Firstly, the sixth-form is going to be very much like the school – except you might not need to wear a uniform. You will be treated as more of a young adult but getting to and from the college will inevitably mean wading through lots of younger pupils. This means that it is always going to feel like a school (even more so if you have already done five years studying there).

However, on the plus side, you can probably walk to it, you won't have to waste time finding your way around and familiarity can be quite a comfort. Plus, you'll be one of the oldest ones there.

School sixth-forms tend to be a little bit smaller than other colleges and again this can have its pluses and minuses. Often school sixth-forms can have a 'family' feel and you will find that you know most of the people in the college. This however means that everyone knows everyone else's business. If you are thinking of asking a classmate out for coffee at the weekend - then the whole college will know about it by Monday morning!

2) A stand-alone sixth-form college

These are usually based in town centres or out-of-town which probably means you are going to need transport to get to it – either a bus or a lift from a family member or friend.

As a stand-alone college you won't have Year 7-11 students, so the place is going to immediately feel older. It also means that on your first day you will once again be the youngest there.

Stand-alone colleges come in various shapes and sizes,

with widely varying academic reputations. Those with good reputations are not going to risk losing it by letting you coast through your time there. Good reputations are fiercely maintained, and this means that you will have to work hard – *sometimes very hard*.

Some colleges actually accept more students than they have places for so that they can have a cull of those that are under-performing. To paraphrase one Principal's first day address: "This is not the place to have fun – this is the place to work hard. You can have fun when you get to university!"

However, if you are fairly academic – you should be able to thrive in this environment and despite what that Principal said, you will have the same social opportunities as other colleges and you will be able to have fun. You will just need more of a 'work hard and play hard' attitude.

Most stand-alone sixth forms will offer more varied subjects - and if you are looking for A Levels that will springboard you into a top university to study science, medicine or law – you might find that a stand-alone sixth-form is better for you.

Of course, not all stand-alone sixth-forms are processing factories for top universities. Some operate more in line with school sixth forms and see personal development as a key objective.

Once again, the smaller stand-alone colleges will have a more 'family' feel whilst those that are bigger tend to encourage the building of friendship groups around subjects rather than college-wide.

3) An FE sixth-form college

Further Education (FE) colleges are slightly different, in that they tend to offer more practical-based subjects via BTECs rather than A Levels. They usually tend to be significantly bigger than other sixth forms and are often split over several campuses (some of which might even be in different towns!)

This means that you are not going to know everyone in the college – in fact you will probably only know the people on your course. An FE college might also offer courses to older students – so on day one you might feel really young as your fellow classmates could be significantly older.

The first thing you will notice is that it is a very grown up environment. There won't be work displays on the wall. You will learn in 'classrooms' that will be used to teach multiple subjects, so expect plain walls, generic seating and a whiteboard. Due to their size, FE colleges tend to not be as strong on the pastoral support or you could find it is managed on another site.

The nature of BTEC subjects also means that they are more coursework-led so teachers and lecturers can track your progress throughout the duration of your course. This means less end-of-course pressure and more onus on you to produce work throughout the year. This makes FE colleges more in line with the work environment compared with academic environments where they might need to push students constantly all the way to the final exams.

Q. How do you apply to sixth form?

Looking at a college's Instagram feed won't give you a feel of what it is like to study there – you need to visit it, listen to the teachers & lecturers, ask questions and decide whether it is for you. Most colleges will start to offer open days during the Autumn term (around October-December).

Remember when you are looking around - it is up to the colleges to impress you rather than the other way around. Yes, that will change when you apply, but at the initial 'choosing' stage you are in control - so make sure whichever college is your first choice – it is the right college for you.

Applying may vary depending on the college. If you are looking to stay on at your school sixth-form then you may need to do nothing other than complete a short form. If you are looking to attend a new sixth-form you will either need to complete a written application form or submit your details online. The specific application process will be explained at the open day or will be available on the college's website.

Q. Should I go to university?

To go or not go?

Believe it or not you don't have to go to university to be successful in life. Jump on Twitter around examination results time and there will be no end of successful business people and celebrities proudly telling you that they didn't go to university. Like all things – it's right for some people and not for others.

It is certainly true that having a degree doesn't guarantee you a job, however in some industries not having a degree will preclude you from successfully applying for certain positions.

If you don't want to go to university – you will find that there are jobs and Apprenticeships available that you could apply for. If you managed to get some A Levels you will find that you are ahead of those that only have GCSE's, however you may also be competing with some people with degrees.

There is also an increasing trend for degree Apprenticeships. Previously, large organisations used to run 'graduate schemes' (where they would employ people straight out of university) but now they are realising that employing someone at 18 means that they can train them and have them up to speed in the job before the 21-year old potential graduate has even taken their exams.

Getting onto a large organisation's degree Apprenticeship programme allows you to study a degree in your own time (alongside your job) which means that you effectively get paid to undertake a degree. These schemes are still in their infancy, but it is easy to see the benefits for employers and how these programmes might ultimately replace graduate scheme programmes.

Q. Is university going to cost me?

One of the main reasons people choose not to go to university is the cost. In 2018, the average cost of a degree was £30,000. This means that someone (either you or your personal benefactor) is going to have to pay for it. If you are lucky and have access to that amount then it will probably be a no-brainer decision to go to university and you can advance straight to choosing a course and a location, but for others the £30,000 price tag can be a real stumbling block.

> *Bear in mind that the average cost includes lots of people who undertake degrees and live in student accommodation in expensive cities as well as those that stay at home and commute daily to their local university. However, with course fees, resources, and associated expenditure, attending any university will have a high cost attached to it.*

Q. How do you pay for university?

Option 1: Getting a student loan

The amount that you can borrow will differ depending on a number of factors including the course you study, the part of the UK you live in (England, Wales, Scotland or Northern Ireland), and your personal circumstances.

As a general rule you can apply for funding as a Student Loan. Student Loans were set up to help people borrow money for university fees and pay it back in small amounts once they start working. How much you pay back is calculated on how much you are earning, but you can expect to accrue interest of around 3% each year. So, if you get a job earning £24,000/year you could expect to pay back £42/month and when you start to earn £30,000, you'll pay back £87/month.

You only start repaying the loan once you earn above a certain salary level (currently £21,000 *August 2019*) and they are cancelled 30 years after you become eligible to repay.

Tuition Fee Loans cover the full cost of the course and are paid straight to the course provider whilst Maintenance Loans are designed to cover your living expenses and these are paid at the start of each term (or monthly in Scotland). The amount you can claim will depend on your household income, where you study, and where you live. You might also be able to apply for grants if you are eligible so it is definitely worth exploring your options. Applications take around six weeks to be processed.

You can find more detailed information via the *www.destination.org.uk/education* page.

Your student loan won't show up on your credit file so it's not going to affect your credit rating (see Money) – but it will be an amount that constantly goes out of your bank account on a monthly basis - and so could be money that you use to save for a house deposit or put towards a car loan.

Option 2: Getting a part-time job

Of course, you don't have to borrow the full amount and you could compliment your fees with a part-time job. Many university towns rely on students to fill roles and this is a good reason to have a great CV (see page 58). Not only will a part-time job provide some much-needed income, but it will also cut down on your free time when you might be tempted to spend money. Whilst most university courses are classed as 'full time' – you might only have 15-20 hours of study per week, and this provides you with lots of time to work in the Student Union or the local coffee shop.

To get a job in a university town, you need to be prepared to walk the streets with a pile of photocopied CVs (these jobs don't always rely on application forms) but if you do this early enough (before other students arrive) you will increase your chances of success.

Option 3: Staying at home and 'commuting'

Fees can also be reduced if you stay at home and 'commute' every day. Since tuition fees were introduced, the number of students staying at home has significantly increased. You might lose part of the 'social experience' of living away but this will be offset by your cheaper living costs – and you can always sleep on a mate's floor if you don't want to go home after a night out.

How far you 'commute' will depend on your access to transport - either your own or public transport such as a bus, tram or train (See Transport). You will be surprised how easily you get into a routine of commuting; even if it takes you an hour to travel door to door. The 'travelling time' will allow you time to think about your studies and if you are on public transport - read up on subjects (or catch up on social media). Invest in a phone with a good battery life and some headphones and you'll grow to love your 'me-time'

Option 4: Delay entry and save up

It is also worth bearing in mind that you don't have to go to university at the age of 18. Most universities accept applications from any age over 18, and it is common for people to have a gap year or 'gap years'. A gap year doesn't have to be spent on a beach in Thailand or travelling the world with a rucksack – it could be spent having a job and building up some savings. This could be particularly useful if you are unsure about whether you want to go to university or are unsure what course you want to study. Either go through the application process and defer your place for twelve months (lots of people do this) or simply decide to apply when you are ready.

Option 5: Bursaries

Finally, if finding the money is too prohibitive, you might find that certain universities offer bursaries, scholarships or can waive fees completely. This is usually done to attract students from low-income families and allows them to demonstrate that they are 'inclusive' to all students. These 'pots of money' are not given away easily – you will need to be able to demonstrate why you should receive it rather than someone else.

You will first need to find the sources of funding that are available and then put a case forward for accessing it. This will start with the question: 'Why should I receive it?'. You will often find details of available funding on the university's website. You will also be able to find out about them at open days – plus this is a great way to make a good first impression and get one hand on any available financial support.

Q. Which university should you choose?

The two main questions here are: 1) Which subject? and 2) Which city or town?

It is probably best to start with the subject. There are lots of websites that will tell you all the places you can study but the first place you should look is UCAS.com. What you will find when you type in a subject – for example 'English Literature' - is a multitude of courses that are all either completely or subtly different. As each university creates its own degree qualifications – there is no standard subject framework for a degree like there is at GCSE or A Level.

This means that you are going to have to do some research to find the course that you want to do. Once you have found your dream course – you will find that the decision 'where to study' has been already made. But choosing a course is only part of the process. You need to go and visit the university, talk to the lecturers, visit the halls of residence and walk around the town to see if it is a place that you can live and study in for three or four years (or possibly even more if you stay after your studies).

Even if you find your dream course and you develop an immediate affiliation for the university you still have to be offered a place. This is why it is useful to have a short list in case things don't work out as they should.

A longer list is also worth considering if you don't have the luxury of being completely mobile (i.e. you can't afford to study in London or commute further than an hour away). If this is the case, you might want to equally consider the subject and location. Here you could type into the search box the subject you are interested in (e.g. English Literature), but immediately disregard those universities that don't meet your criteria - whatever that is. Even if you are very specific about the location you may find that your chosen university still has a number of similar courses that you can chose from.

It is also important to look at the syllabus for the full duration of the course (particularly in Years 2 and 3), as many courses can be customisable to something you have a real interest in. This could mean that you can choose a university in a 'cheaper' area but still get to study elements that you initially thought were only available elsewhere.

Like all important decisions, the more effort you put in, the better the result will be. Whilst lots of people will be on hand to help you (family, friends, sixth-form teachers/lecturers, university lecturers/admissions officers, online reviews) the person that will be affected the most by the decision is you – so it is in your best interests to get it right.

How do you apply for university?

The formal process starts in Year 13 at sixth-form, but there is nothing to say that it can't start before then. The key date for your diary is the end of January (nine months before your potential start date) when you will need to have your UCAS application form submitted. This is unless you are applying for Oxford or Cambridge or other courses that have an early UCAS deadline of mid-October.

Prior to these dates, you will have the opportunity to research courses, draw up a short list, attend university open days, and pull together a CV/Application Form that will require a personal statement that defines you in around 200 words.

You have from the start of September to the end of January. This is five months to sort the most important decision of your life to date. Yet for most people, they will still be completing the application form minutes before the final deadline.

Some universities (such as Oxford and Cambridge) may have an entrance exam & interview to short list applicants. If you think completing an application form is hard work – you should feel the pressure when a university professor starts interviewing and interrogating you about the subject you want to study.

Even if you aren't 100% certain you are going to go to university, it is worth applying and having the option later on. The worse thing you can do is not apply and then decide to in the summer when all the best courses have been filled.

Why is the LifeLocation® Education important?

As a teen and young adult it is your education and qualifications that define how you progress to the next level.

They demonstrate to sixth-form colleges and universities whether or not you will be able to undertake the courses that they offer and they will provide an indication to employers as to the level of work you can handle.

For those that flourish in education, you will find that there is no limit in what you can achieve, however if you haven't maximised your education potential you might want to consider re-enrolling.

Without doubt the singularly most important thing as a teen and young adult is to ensure that you have qualifications in English and maths. Without these you will find reaching your Destination Adulthood is very difficult.

Further Links

www.destination.org.uk - *Lots of specially commissioned and curated content relating to education choices and information*

Check your **local authority website** for lists of schools and colleges in your area

www.UCAS.com - *Information on degree courses and*

applying for universities

www.thestudentroom.co.uk - *Information about university life*

Resetting your education journey

Soft or Factory Resets

- **Picked the wrong sixth-form or FE college?** You can easily change colleges – look on their websites for more details
- **Not sure whether university is right for you?** Why not attend some open days and/or ask people who have been there and done it
- **Not got the exam results you need or feel you deserved?** – Then why not enrol at a local college – either full time or as an evening course.
- **Always hated school and left with no qualifications?** – It's time to reset, dig deep and force yourself back into education. Start by attending some local college open evenings. It might be that you are dyslexic or have another condition that prevents you from easily learning. Addressing and understanding this will make studying easier. No one is going to say it is going to be easy – but getting back in the education game could be one of the best decisions you ever make. Discuss your requirements with a local college – you'll be amazed at how much they'll want to help you.

LifeLocation® 2. Employment

Q. Will this be decided in my Careers Advice?

The amount and quality of careers advice that you can expect to receive will vary depending on where you live as responsibility for careers advice now falls with local councils.

Whilst the National Careers Service (funded by Government) operates a detailed support website, formal careers support (i.e. where you get to talk one-to-one to an expert) is often quite minimal.

Lately, the role of careers advice has been picked up by schools and colleges, with many now offering some form of adviser service.

If you were planning to rely on a careers adviser to find you a career - don't!

Having a service is one thing – advising on specific careers is another, as advisers simply don't have the knowledge to know about every job that exists.

Let's assume for example you want a career in television. In the first instance it is probably safe to assume that your careers adviser won't have 40 years' experience in the television industry. Watch any TV programme and during the credits at the end you will see a list of potential jobs that exist in the industry (and these are just the production-based ones).

Within the industry there are big players like the BBC or ITV but there are also thousands of small service companies ranging from independent production houses, outdoor catering companies through to those selling on-screen advertising. There isn't anyone in the country who can break all these roles and companies down and tell you the exact route to gaining a career in them. And this is just television – there are literally hundreds of industry sectors, with multiple jobs and organisations within each one.

Careers advice as a service comes from a past era when the process was much simpler and sectors had pre-defined ways of entering them. You wanted to get into banking – start at the bottom in a branch and work your way up. You want to become an accountant – apply to be an account assistant, do your exams and work your way up. You want to get a job in TV, find someone who will give you a job on a film shoot as a runner (making coffees, running errands etc) and work your way up. In the past, very few jobs involved technology, but with the internet and digital communications taking over, jobs have significantly changed. Your phone probably has more processing power than a computer from the year you were born. This has created a whole new raft of jobs that previously didn't exist; thousands of which your average careers adviser knows nothing about.

Like everything, if you want to know about it – you need to take the responsibility yourself and find it out. You are part of the first generation that has 'Google' at its fingertips and the ability to discover anything within a few clicks.

What you might then be able to use your time with a careers adviser for is advice on applying for a job, making sure your CV is up to scratch and providing you with some interview tips. Just don't expect them to sort your career for you.

CVs and Application forms

Back in the past, a CV was a double-sided sheet of A4 where you recorded all the important information relevant to getting a job: your qualifications, the schools and colleges you attended, work experience, your hobbies and details of your references.

CVs are still useful in pulling all your information into one place, but because there was never a standard format, it was difficult for recruiters to compare candidates. Many organisations now prefer to use an application form which uses questions related to the specific job vacancy.

Within this book we will often use the phrase CV and this relates to your specific set of skills and experiences rather than the specific two sided document.

Q. What can you tell me about Apprenticeships

So, you don't fancy being in education any more. Fine, no problem but you are going to need to get a job.

You will probably be aware of Apprenticeships. These are full time jobs that combine 'on-the-job' work experience with formal training that results in a qualification (usually a BTEC). Apprenticeships are defined by the level of qualification that is attained. Level 2 Apprenticeships come with a Level 2 qualification, a Level 3 Apprenticeship comes with a Level 3 qualification and so on. If you struggled at school then you might want to start with a Level 2, however if you were okay at school but you didn't fancy doing A Levels, you might want to jump straight into a Level 3.

As a rough guide, a Level 2 is pitched at the same academic level as a GCSE, whereas a Level 3 is more similar to an A Level. Therefore, if you struggled with GCSE's you might to find a Level 2 difficult – however if you work hard (and remember this isn't school) it is still achievable.

If you are struggling to get a Level 2 apprenticeship due to your qualifications or circumstances you might want to consider a Traineeship. A Traineeship is a course with work experience that gets you ready for an Apprenticeship or into work. It's unpaid but you may receive expenses for meals and travel. Not being paid might not sound great but this might be a necessary to go 'one step back to go two steps forward'. Just imagine what Apprenticeship or work opportunities might be available once you have completed a Traineeship and gained some work experience.

One of the main things to bear in mind with an Apprenticeship is that you can't just start one when you fancy it. It has to be attached to a job position and therefore in most cases you need to apply and get the job before you can start it.

It is a fact that there are more people looking for a job or an Apprenticeship than there are vacancies. This means you have to consider that if you do find your dream position (or even just a position that is *'meh'*) – there will be lots of people applying for it – and only one person will be successful.

Applying for jobs is where all the hard work getting a good CV will pay off. When 50 people apply for an Apprenticeship – the employer will make the first decision based on the qualifications, work experience and extra-curricular activities of the applicants.

Employing staff is a really difficult decision for an employer and they will have many sleepless nights worrying about making the right choice. As a result, those responsible for recruiting staff will try to reduce the risk and make the process as easy as possible.

A packed CV or application form full of additional activities shows the employer that this potential employee doesn't sit around all day and has a number of varied interests.

This enables the recruiter to build an instant picture of the applicant. Compare this with an application where the candidate supplies no additional information and it is a no-brainer – the full CV will win every day. If your application is the sparse one – then you could be saying goodbye to your dream job!

Q. How do you get an Apprenticeship?

Getting an Apprenticeship is going to require some effort. Even before you start to worry about whether your CV is up to scratch, you are going to have to find a vacancy. There is no set way that companies advertise jobs. Some will advertise in the local newspaper, some will post the position online (via job sites) and some will use their own website and social media. This is in addition to those that go directly to the local college, the Apprenticeship training provider or those that simply rely having a large number of speculative applicants already on file.

This means that if you are serious about getting an Apprenticeship – you need a plan.

Firstly, you need to get an idea of the type of Apprenticeship and the level that you will be studying at.

A good place to start is by looking at the Apprenticeship GetInGoFar.gov.uk website (Scotland & Wales have their own - see page 86). This will have a list of all the vacancies in your area and give you an idea of the roles available.

You can also sign up to the site and get useful tips and information on getting an Apprenticeship.

It will really help if you can narrow down the type of Apprenticeship you want. For example, if you want to work in animal care or hospitality (or any sector), try and identify the companies locally that might offer Apprenticeships (or have done so previously). By doing this, you could write to the company and ask about any potential vacancies now or in the future. You might not hear back immediately, but it might be that they keep your details on file and add you to their speculative applicant list.

Getting an Apprenticeship is a proactive process (i.e. something you have to be responsible for). You might also want to follow potential employers, colleges, and Apprenticeship training providers on social media. Remember to keep your CV up to date so that as soon as a vacancy is made available you are ready to apply for it.

Q. What will help me get an Apprenticeship?

If you are interested in a specific career sector – try and get some experience in it. If you want to work in digital marketing – there is nothing to stop you contacting some local digital marketing companies and asking if you could do some work experience. You never know – if you impress them sufficiently, they might even offer you a job or an Apprenticeship!

One thing that you need to be aware of is that you are not just competing against people your own age and with similar qualifications and experience. People can start an Apprenticeship at any age, and it is now a common route for those finishing GCSEs, those with A Levels who don't want to go to university and it is also not uncommon for those who drop out of university to seek an Apprenticeship or those with a degree who are struggling to find work.

This means that competition for a Level 3 Apprenticeship could include someone with GCSEs, someone with A Levels and someone with a degree. Put yourself in the position of the employer and think about who you would employ – the sixteen-year old with no experience or the 21 year-old with an extra five years of 'maturing' behind them? However, the flip side of this is that an employer might specifically want someone who is younger that can be moulded into a role within the company. Every job is different – and as a result you need to use your unique strengths to ensure that the recruiter thinks you are a better candidate than the competition.

This is another reason for finding the vacancy before it is advertised – the more people that are aware of the job and subsequently applying, means that the odds of you being successful are lower.

The final point to make about an Apprenticeship (*or any job really*) is that getting the position is nowhere near as hard as keeping it. From day one, your employer is going to expect you to work as hard as all the other employees (despite the fact that you could be earning the least). You will obviously be given some slack initially - in that they will know that it is your first job (and a large part of an Apprenticeship is about learning *how to work*) - but if you constantly turn up late, make mistakes, or take lots of single days off ill, you won't have an Apprenticeship for very long. Always remember how many other people applied for your job – and how many of them would love to step into your shoes if you mess up!

Q. How can I get the best job I can?

Whether you decide to get a job at 16 or are putting it off as long as you can – at some point you are going to have to suck it up and join the 45 million people that are employed within the UK.

A wise person once said: "do a job that you like, and you'll never work a day in life" and this is very true. However, there are a large proportion of people who do a job every day that they don't enjoy.

Many of these people report that they just fell into the job as there was nothing else available or that they didn't know what to do. This is not to say that they dislike their jobs. There are many other factors that have to be taken into account about a job – its location, its hours, the number of holidays that people get, whether the staff are friendly, and/or the daily stress levels. Working in a call centre might not be your first choice of job, but for many it's a low-pressure role where they can have a good laugh with their colleagues.

Most full-time jobs last about 40 hours/week which is over 2,000 hours/year. Add in the travel time and you'll find that you are spending more time at work than you are playing sports, socialising with your mates or playing on your phone. Imagine spending 2,000 hours on an old phone with no internet access. That's what it's like to do something you don't enjoy.

The big advantage when you are young is that you have every job in the world to choose from – the only thing holding you back is your determination to get it.

Deciding on a career

At some point you are going to have to make a decision on what you want to do.

The first thing to do is to think about the things you enjoy doing and the things that you are good at. Don't be too literal with this. You might enjoy playing football, but it is unlikely that you will become a professional footballer. However, there are hundreds of jobs that involve football. These might vary from being a club physiotherapist, someone who interviews the players for the club programme, the groundsperson who looks after the pitch or person who runs the ticket office. You could even look at working for the local football association or getting a job at Wembley Stadium.

This is when you then start to look at the other skills and interests you have. "Are you good at English?", "What is your maths like?", "Would you prefer to work inside or outside?" It is impossible to list every job that exists (or even just list all the jobs that are available in and around football.) This is your career and taking the responsibility to put in a bit of hard work at the start will pay dividends in the future.

Start by doing some research. 30 years ago, this meant having to go to a library – but now you have every library in the world in the palm of your hands. Grab your phone, open up your internet browser and type "Jobs in Football" (or whichever subject you are interested in) and look at what is available. You might not see your dream job, but it might just open your eyes to the type of jobs that you might want to do and what skills or qualifications you will need to get a job in this field.

As you undertake your research and start to find potential careers that you can see yourself doing, you might discover that you don't meet all the requirements of the role. Some jobs will require a degree, some a BTEC qualification and some may expect you to have experience of working in the sector. Don't be put off if you don't have what they are asking for – instead treat it as a 'tick list' of the things that you are going to need to get that job in the future.

> *Remember you are at the start of your working journey and you don't have to do one job for your whole life.*

The key is to set goals that you can aim for. For example,

if you need a degree for your dream job but don't fancy going to university, then how about finding a degree Apprenticeship in a similar role that will allow you to get the qualification you need? Sure, it might take you twice as long to get your qualification, but you are probably going to be working until you are 65/70 years of age anyway, so a few years spent getting the relevant skills is a small price to pay. Just imagine – a bit of hard work now and you could be doing a job that you love for 40/45 years and getting paid to do it.

The other advantage in building your skills now is that you have time to look at all the companies you'd like to work for and build your networks within them. Employers like to see candidates who have an interest in their vacancies so anything that you can do to demonstrate your interest will get you noticed. You could start by asking for work experience or volunteering opportunities. Getting your dream job is a long game – and one that you are going to need a shark-like laser focus to succeed in.

Q. Why is having a good CV important?

Whatever job you are applying for, you are going to need a great CV – and the only person who can make it 'pop' is you.
Again, this is not the time to feel sorry for yourself. There will always be someone who has done and achieved more. But so what? The only thing that matters to you, is you.

So how do you make it 'pop'. Let's start with qualifications. Obviously we can't do anything about them in the short-term, but in the world of applying for jobs they provide the main indicator to an employer of the level of work you can deliver.

Every job has a minimum qualification level. If you don't meet that level, you have a simple choice – 1) Get more qualifications and apply in a few years when you have them or 2) Apply for something you are more qualified for.

Remember, the qualifications that you have is not a locked down list – you can always add more, and people do this all the time throughout their lives

At this point it is important to remind you that you really need to have a minimum GCSE in English and maths. If you don't – and you only do one thing as a result of reading this book – you should enrol at a college and work your butt off to get them.

Nothing will potentially hold you back more than not having an English and maths qualification – and as much as you might want to blame everyone else and have an armful of excuses why you don't – the only person responsible for not having a basic qualification in English and/or maths is you.

Q. How do I stand out from the competition?

So, assuming that your skills and qualifications meet the job requirements - the next stage is to ensure that you stand out above the competition (i.e. the other applicants). But how do you do this? Two areas that you can do this are:
1) Work Experience
2) Extra-curricular activities

1) Work Experience

Every employer wants to know two things: 1) that you will be able to do the job, and 2) that you are not going to leave after a week (and therefore they aren't going to have to go through the whole costly and time-consuming recruitment process again).

This is why you need to show your potential employer that you are a safe pair of hands and that it wouldn't be a risk to employ you.

The first way you can do this is by showing them that you have undertaken some form of work experience. Ideally this will be related to the job you are applying for, however if you can demonstrate 'transferable skills' (i.e. an accumulation of life skills that are relevant for a variety of roles such as time keeping, dealing with responsibilities etc) and the skills listed in the Life Skills LifeLocation®, then this will impress the recruiter.

For example, if you undertook a week's work experience in an office and one of the tasks was dealing with money, what you instantly demonstrate to an employer is that you are trustworthy and have a good attention to detail. Add to this that you were on time every day, was always polite, you were able to work without having your phone switched on, and that the office manager said that they would give you a reference, and you have a week of your life that was really well spent. This says so much more to an employer than someone who has no experience of work at all.

> *"But it's not fair my school/college didn't do work experience."*

Again, it's important to get rid of the excuses. That was then, this is now, and you are working towards getting a job in the future.

If you don't have any work experience on your CV then you need to take the initiative and try and get some.

Why not Identify some companies (maybe local companies or ones where family or friends work) and either pick up the phone or go into reception and ask if they offer work experience. If they do, ask "how would I apply?"

You could email them but this isn't a suggested option. Whilst it's easy to fire off 10 emails and then wait for a response, it is just as easy for emails to go to the wrong address or be ignored by the recipient. Standing in reception immediately suggests that you are keen – it also means that you can ask the receptionist for the name of the correct person to deal with.

> *Top Tip: If you are going to go into a reception, you need to make sure that you have prepared what you are going to say in your head beforehand.*
>
> *Something like this: "Hello, I am really keen to work in an organisation like [name of company] but I don't have any work experience on my CV. Would it be possible to speak to the person who deals with work experience or tell me how I would apply?"*

You might get brushed off 9 times out of 10, but when you get the 1 it will be worth it, and you will feel like an absolute boss.

Employers like to see determination and initiative, and nothing shows it more than a young person knocking on doors looking for a chance to impress.

2) Extra Curricular Activities

If you don't fancy knocking on doors, you could always offer to volunteer in your local community. Most areas have a variety of opportunities ranging from working in the hospice shop, helping out at a sports club, or maintaining local environmental areas.

Organisations wishing to utilise volunteers rely on one key aspect – that the volunteers will in some way be interested and engaged with the product or service that they offer. Every Saturday morning around 10,000 people throughout the UK volunteer to support one of the 500+ Parkruns. Most of the volunteers are people who are interested in running and want to help provide a facility for other runners. If you aren't interested in the 'thing' being offered, it's unlikely that you will get the warm and fuzzy selfless feeling that helping out creates.

There are many areas that people can volunteer in. The key is to find one that you are interested in. Once you have decided, getting involved is usually easy – simply make contact and go from there. You might even be able to do it with a friend so it's a lot less daunting. It's unlikely you'll get the best jobs on day one, but if you continue to go and give up a little bit of your time on a regular basis, you will soon reap the rewards and become a valuable member of the team.

Volunteering also has the advantage that you get to meet new friends and therefore make new contacts. Many people who volunteer also have full-time jobs and meeting new people is an opportunity to extend your network and get the inside knowledge on potential jobs and other opportunities before they are advertised.

Again, nothing is guaranteed, but a period of volunteering will certainly do better to enhance your CV than doing nothing will.

By knowing your skill shortages, you can use work experience and volunteering to fill the gaps. If you haven't done a lot of team-working – then a collective litter-pick along a local canal will tick that box. If you need experience of customer service – helping out with meals at a local care home is a great idea.

When you apply for a job, the person who is responsible for filling the position will have a sheet of paper with a grid printed on it, listing all the skills that they believe the ideal candidate will possess. These will include team-working, customer service, etc. For each of these sections they will scour your CV and/or your application form and give you a score based on the level of expertise and experience that you have. Each section's score will then be added up to give a total. The highest will then be invited to interview, the lowest will be discarded. It is therefore up to you to make sure that you score high in each section.

The hard part is that often you don't know the sections they will be scoring on – but if you know what skills are required for the job – you should have a good idea of what they will be looking for.

Q. How do I deliver a great job interview?

Your work experience and volunteering activities are also key parts of what are known as 'interview fillers' - things you can talk about in an interview. The interview is the opportunity for an employer to meet you and assess whether you will fit into the company. Despite what people might say – everyone is nervous in an interview and sometimes this can mean that things get a bit ... *awkward*.

This isn't just for the person being interviewed, it applies to the interviewer too. There is nothing more difficult than when you ask a question to a candidate and it doesn't gain a response, or if there is simply nothing to talk to a candidate about. An interview is about trying to generate a conversation and to do this it requires questions *and* answers.

> *Believe me, the interviewer is desperate to get a conversation going as it: a) will give them an opportunity to correctly assess the candidate and b) ensure that it isn't 30 minutes of absolute silent torture!*

Having interesting (and different) things to talk about are brilliant for interviewers as it means they get to ask interesting and different questions. "Oh I see you did some work experience at the local cinema ... tell me about that. What did you do? What type of cinema was it? What shifts did you do? Who did you report to? What was the best part of it? Do you like films? What's your favourite?"

That's over half of the interview right there - and you are answering questions on something that you know about. If you can sound confident, polite, and knowledgeable – you are well on your way to getting that job. You are certainly much nearer than the person who has done nothing, has nothing to say and is sat in silence.

Q. What is the best type of organisation for me?

As well as choosing the type of job that you might want, you also need to consider the type of organisation that you want to work in and which might be best for you.

Businesses come in a variety of shapes and sizes and each role and organisation will have what is known as a 'culture'. A culture is best described as the way that people behave within the organisation. For example, some industry sectors (recruitment, advertising, corporate finance) are highly competitive and staff are put under lots of pressure to deliver results. This means that staff often have to work long hours in the office with some 'workplace cultures' frowning on people who don't work a twelve-hour day. Now often these long days are rewarded with high pay (or 'fun' offices with bars and slides) but they aren't ideal if you want to eat an evening meal with your family at 5.30pm.

On the flip-side, some organisations have a more laid-back culture and have flexible hours but they tend to be staffed by older workers who don't want a high-pressure job. However, in these organisations you will still be expected to do your job very well within the hours that you work.

Some organisations rely on people staying outside of their contracted hours in order to benefit others (e.g. nurses), whilst some rely on people staying late for the benefit of profits. Again, it will be important to select a role and a company that motivates you and is aligned to the lifestyle and the Destination Adulthood that you want to reach.

Despite what people say there aren't any easy jobs. There are however jobs that you will enjoy and companies you will enjoy working for and this will make the job feel significantly easier.

There are three main types of organisations:
- Private Sector
- Public Sector
- Voluntary sector

Private Sector Organisations

This wide-ranging title covers the organisations that might be classed as businesses – i.e. companies that sell things and try to make a financial profit. They will range from sole traders, small businesses, through to multi-national businesses with thousands of staff.

Whether you are working in a small or large company you will be expected to contribute to the success of the business. Even if you are on a management fast-track programme within a supermarket or construction company and starting at the bottom (whether its on the tills or labouring on a building site) – you will be expected to not make mistakes that will cost money and be part of a well-oiled company machine that is doing everything it can to be successful.

Within a smaller company you will be more exposed, and it is more likely that you will have direct contact with the business owner. This is good in the respect that they will get to know you and will be keen to develop you as a key member of the business, however it could be bad in that your mistakes will be noticed throughout the company. Within a bigger organisation it is easier to hide and find your feet as you will be reporting to a manager rather than the business owner.

You will also find that a bigger company will have more rules and structures in place. As an example, within a big company you will probably start with a week-long induction that will take you around each aspect of the business. You will also find that all the legal paperwork is in place and your job will mirror almost exactly your job description. A small company however might be more informal and ad-hoc. Your induction might consist of a half-hour chat and then you will be straight into the job. You will also probably be asked to do a variety of jobs (often with little notice) but this will mean that you will gain lots of new skills and experience in a much shorter time.

You will also find that if you work hard in a smaller company

– you can progress much quicker. In a larger company, recruitment will be more formal (with vacancies offered to external as well as internal candidates).

A smaller company will be much more proactive in seeking opportunities and a new piece of work could easily be given to you if you have demonstrated your ability. A larger company will be much more consistent and as a result you will find yourself doing the same job for longer.

Zero Hours Contracts

Of late, zero-hours contracts have become very popular with employers. To a business they are ideal in that they only have to pay a zero-hours contracted employee for the hours that they work.

For some employees they work really well in that they allow the person to control when they work and take advantage of overtime when they want to earn extra income. It also allows people to have more than one job and therefore have the security that they aren't relying on one company for employment. However, for most they aren't ideal as a main income contract as the varying monthly amount doesn't allow them to budget consistently.

As we will see in Money, one of the core shifts from being a teen to a young adult is having responsibility for a weekly or monthly budget and this is very difficult to do if you don't have a consistent amount.

Public Sector

If you were starting work in a public sector organisation thirty years ago, you would have found a relaxed workplace without the pressures of having to make a profit.

Instead of selling things, public sector organisations are funded by Government to provide beneficial products and services to the population. These types of organisations include the NHS, local authorities, the Prison Service and many more. You could also add universities, colleges and schools to this list but the increasing competition between these organisations, has forced them to operate more as private sector organisations.

However, as austerity cuts have taken effect, Government spending in these areas has been significantly decreased. This has largely affected the number of people employed by public sector organisations though it hasn't decreased the amount of work that is required. This means that fewer people are expected to deliver more work.

Large numbers of people work in the public sector because they are motivated by the concept of 'public service' i.e. delivering products and services that benefit individuals and communities. Whereas in the private sector – people might put in the extra effort in the hope of a financial benefit, within the private sector people put in the extra effort knowing that somewhere, somebody's life will be improved.

Temporary or Fixed-term contracts

A trend of public sector organisations are temporary or fixed-term contracts. Because public sector organisations are funded through Government finances, they often only receive funding for projects with a limited time-span. This is because in theory after a set time the project will have solved the problem it set out to fix. Rather than employ someone on a full-time contract (i.e. they have a job until it is formally terminated – either by the employer or the employee resigning) they offer a fixed term contract.

This means you only have a guaranteed job for a limited time period (e.g. 6 months, one year, or three years etc.). This has the massive benefit for organisations that they don't have to employ someone once the money runs out. In reality, many public sector organisations are constantly looking for new projects (and new sources of funding) and as a result people often jump from one fixed-term contract to another.

However, whilst a fixed-term three year contract with a public sector organisation offers a period of job security, this is not a view necessarily shared by financial lenders such as banks. Banks want to ensure that you are going to be able to pay a loan or mortgage for the full duration of the term, but if you can only guarantee an income for a proportion of it – the bank may reject your application. Ironically, a full-time position is often seen as more secure even though a company could terminate your employment at any time.

Of course these contracts also have positives. If you have a belief in the concept of public service you will want to maximise the limited time period and achieve the objectives that have been defined by the project. Once these objectives have been reached, you are then free to look at other projects that match your experience and your specific interests.

Voluntary sector

This sector is largely dominated by charities, but it is increasingly seeing growth from organisations who are setting up with a social purpose and who use their profits to benefit the causes that they are interested in.

The charity sector is undoubtedly a competitive one and it tends to recruit people who are passionate about a specific cause. Whilst at the front end, volunteers may be relied upon to run shops or promote activities, but behind them are often large structured organisations staffed by professional, well-paid employees. Working for a charity or an organisation with a social purpose doesn't necessarily mean that you won't get paid, nor will you not be able to take advantage of a full-time contract. Not all money raised by charities goes to the cause – a proportion is kept to fund 'running costs' of which one of the largest single amounts will be employee wages.

A good way to get into the sector is to initially volunteer and then work your way into a paid position.

Q. What do I need to consider about a job?

You are likely to be working for around 40 to 50 years. As a result it is important to do something in that time that you are going to enjoy. The salary that you start on is unlikely to be the salary you will have when you finish.

These are the things that you need to consider before diving into a job or career:

Salary - What salary are you looking to earn?

Bear in mind that the higher the salary, the more likely you will be working longer hours, possibly working away from home more and/or have more responsibility and pressure.

Your salary will dictate the property that you live in, where it is and how close it is to your workplace and your friends and family. Your salary will also dictate the lifestyle that you have outside of work: where you go on holiday, the supermarket that you shop in and the type of clothes that you wear.

Of course, at some point you may share your income with a partner (and vice versa) or you may have to stop working for a period to raise children. These are all aspects that you need to consider.

You need to also look at the rest of the 'package'. This will include benefits that are in addition to the salary. These benefits might include: how many days holiday you get (the standard is 28 including bank holidays); whether or not they are paying into a pension for you (legally they should offer you a pension but they don't necessarily have to pay into it if you are earning a low amount). In addition, it might also include medical insurance, use of a car/van, or even giving you your own computer. Every job and organisation will be different so it is worth looking at all aspects of the job salary and package.

Career Progression

Is the job going to allow you to progress within it? Does the company have a career ladder that you can envisage climbing or will you have to leave the company to progress? If you want to progress, is the job going to help you achieve this? Will the job be a stepping stone or will it be something that you'll be embarrassed about on your CV?

Sector Success vs. the threat of AI

Are you going into a job and/or company that is on the up? Is the organisation successful (in which case will they become more successful?) Or are they struggling? Is the sector still going to exist in ten years or will it be superseded by technology? What is the future of your job role? Does it have the potential to be replaced by a robot or outsourced to a company overseas?

The last thing you want to do is pour your life and hard work into a job that isn't going to exist in a few years.

Can you do the job?

Have you got what it takes to do the job? If the post involves writing – are your English skills up to scratch? Likewise, if you are going to work with numbers – are your maths skills adequate? Are you personable? Do you like working away from home? Do you like driving? Do you like sitting on a phone talking to strangers? Can you work outdoors in winter? Can you show empathy to a customer who needs your help? Every job requires a different set of skills – do you have the skills needed for your dream job?

If you don't have the skills (or interest in developing them) which would enable you to do the job – you might be best giving this specific role a wide berth.

Training

Is the company going to help you become the best version of you? Will they constantly train you and equip you with new skills? Will they support you to gain extra qualifications that are going to help you progress? Do they have a culture of developing their employees?

Working for an organisation that is going to invest in your development is a good sign that they value their employees.

Q. Will I enjoy my job?

50 years is a long time to do the same thing. Sure, you can leave and change jobs or companies at any time, but the reality is that many people don't – *even super cool millennials!* People get into a job, get used to the salary and find very quickly that they have refined their skills to that specific job. This means that people get pigeon-holed into a certain career and it is very difficult to pack it in and do something completely different.

Yes, it's do-able to change career and do something different, but it's not easy. It's much easier to start doing something you enjoy at the beginning and start building a career from there.

Why is the LifeLocation® Employment important?

At some point we all need to get a job but there are many routes to getting one.

The increasing competition for roles means that you need to have a full armoury prepared to ensure you are successful.

Apprenticeships are a great way to get your foot in the door but so can a graduate position.

The key is to find the best route for you and ensure that you have a full CV with lots of work experience and extracurriculum activity.

Just remember, getting a job is hard but keeping it is even harder.

Further Links

www.destination.org.uk - *Lots of specially commissioned and curated content relating to employment choices and information*

Check your **local authority website** for lists of local apprenticeship opportunities and employment programmes in your area

National Careers Service (England)
www.nationalcareersservice.direct.gov.uk
Careers Wales
www.careerswales.com
My world of work (Scotland)
www.myworldofwork.co.uk

Apprenticeships (England)
www.apprenticeships.org.uk (factual information)
www.GetInGoFar.gov.uk (more user friendly)
Apprenticeships (Scotland)
www.apprenticeships.scot
Apprenticeships (Wales)
www.gov.wales/apprenticeships-skills-and-training (Wales)

Youth Employment UK
www.youthemployment.org.uk

Apprenticeship Guide
www.apprenticeshipguide.co.uk

notgoingtouni – Advertising heavy but some useful information on large Apprenticeship providers
www.notgoingtouni.co.uk

Also consider **job recruitment sites** such as: Milkround, Indeed, Glassdoor, Reed, jobsite.co.uk, Monster, totaljobs and fish4.

Resetting your employment options

Soft and Factory Resets

- **No idea of what to do as a career?** Why not think about your hobbies or the things you enjoy? – Think about all the different jobs that are involved – do you have any of the skills required for these roles?
- **Don't have any previous experience?** – Why not consider some volunteering or unpaid work to get your foot in the door?
- **Apprenticeship not working out?** Are you in a job that you don't like? It's never too late to consider a change of career.
- **Are you unemployed?** Do you feel that you are already on the scrapheap? – You need to give yourself

an honest talking to and hunt out some support that is going to help you get into employment. Start with either your local careers service, your Job Centre or contact or your local into-work programme.

LifeLocation® 3. Life Skills

Q. What Life Skills do I need?

Having the right skills are essential if you are to successfully navigate the journey from a teen to an adult.

Qualifications are obviously important, but they do not tell the whole story about someone. In fact, they are fairly limited in what they show, other than that a person learnt 'something' to a 'certain academic level'.

As you progress through life you will find that people are less bothered about the grades and the actual qualifications you attained and instead it will be your life skills that will be judged and evaluated.

Life skills are essentially all the qualities and abilities that you have but that you don't get a certificate for. With more people wanting jobs than there are positions available, the number of applicants for each vacancy is often really high. In these cases it means that employers can be very fussy about who they employ and they can compare multiple candidates without just having to rely on their qualifications.

Youth Employment UK are an organisation that works closely with employers and uses this knowledge to help young people understand what is required to get into work. They undertook a large survey with employers and the results showed the five key life and work skills that employers are looking for:
- Communication
- Teamwork
- Problem Solving
- Self Management
- Self Belief

But it is not just employers who benefit from having employees with these skills - you will too. Having these skills as a young adult will help in a variety of situations, not just in the workplace. They will also be invaluable in helping you reach your Destination Adulthood.

Communication

Communication isn't just about talking, it's also about listening, body language and being able to get across your thoughts, ideas and opinions.

Being a good communicator doesn't mean that you can just 'nail' presentations. Communication skills are used in lots of different ways within your working life including reading, writing, note taking, writing reports, and briefing colleagues & managers. These skills will also help in your personal life too; in areas such as meeting new people, ringing your bank to query something on a statement or completing an insurance claim form if someone has crashed into your car.

Your English skills (in particular using correct spellings and grammar) will say a great deal about you. In a world with 'spell-check', nothing you produce should really be going out spelt incorrectly. Nothing will undermine you quicker than a piece of writing full of errors. No one ever won a debate on social media with posts full of 'typos' - just as a CV or application form with spelling errors is the quickest way to not get an interview. This might not sound fair if it's not one of your strengths, but sadly it's what happens in reality.

As with all skills, communication skills are only improved by practice. Why not try a mock job interview at home or even make your own YouTube video? You can guarantee that the first one will make you cringe, but the more you prepare and the more you practice, the better you will get.

You could also start to write. Why not write a 100 word review of this book, a film or box-set you've just watched? Again, the more you do it, the better it will become. Plus you never know, you might get good at it and start your own blog or website.

> *As I said on page 16, I originally failed English GCSE and I knew that I had to get better at it. A friend suggested that I should write for the college newspaper and so I wrote my first public piece of writing - a review of a Madonna concert I had*

attended. It was about 200 words and it took me about a week to write (and rewrite) before I was happy with it.

But I did it and it was published. This gave me the confidence to write more and at university I became the music editor on the university magazine.

Through pushing myself I improved my English skills and companies now pay me to write on their behalf.

Teamwork

As much as some people might think they are a superhero – no one can do everything. Most things in life involve the contribution of multiple people and it is important that you have the skills to work in a group.

Within a workplace you will have: a) people that you will rely on to do your job, and b) people who will rely on you to do their job. Working together and solving problems collectively is much more effective than trying to do everything individually.

Very few workplace tasks exist in isolation. If you work in a racehorse yard, you will need to work with the stable manager and plan your day around deliveries, when the jockey might want to take the horses out, feeding times etc. You simply cannot come in at 9.00am and do the jobs when you want to do them. By working as a 'team' you are much more effective and the overall job is delivered much more successfully.

Communication skills are key in team-working. You will need to listen to what other team members are saying and be able to understand it and apply it to your own tasks. By understanding how all the roles interact you will be able to shape and improve how you work.

Team working isn't always easy. Some people will try to delegate all their tasks and sometimes you will need to be firm in pointing out the reasons why you can't do them. This might be difficult if the other person is more senior, but the last thing that the group want is for you to accept more tasks if you are unable to deliver.

Problem Solving

Being able to deal with problems is an important skill, just as not being able to solve problems can have major consequences both in life and in the workplace.

- If your car breaks down on the motorway – what do you do?
- You accidentally send an inappropriate email to your boss – what are you going to do?
- You get a customer complaining – what are you going to do?

If your answer to any of the above questions was to curl up in a ball and wait for it to pass – then you need to sharpen your problem-solving skills.

The first thing you need to know is that most problems can

be overcome - you just need to have a positive mindset. If you believe that it can be solved, you are halfway there. You now just need to find a way of solving it.

One way is to use this handy 5-point plan:
- What is the problem?
- What can I do to solve it?
- Select the best option
- Attempt to solve the problem
- Identify whether the problem was solved

Anticipating that a problem might happen and preparing for the worse is one way of dealing with things. Being aware of the things that could go wrong and actively ensuring that they don't happen, is always the best way to solve a problem.

Here are ways you could have solved the problems mentioned on the previous page:
- Being a member of a roadside recovery service such as the AA means that your car breakdown can be dealt with in one telephone call
- Double checking email recipients before sending will always ensure that emails are only sent to the correct people
- Being aware of the company procedure for dealing with customer complaints will ensure you deal correctly with tricky confrontations

Honesty is always the best policy. Owning up if you are in the wrong is often the best way to stop a problem escalating. Likewise, sharing the problem with a friend or colleague might help produce a satisfactory outcome. Alternatively, being able to quickly consider multiple options and their potential outcomes and actioning accordingly will allow you to solve the problem in the most effective way possible.

Self Management

Self management is about taking responsibility for your own actions and ensuring that you do things to the best of your ability. It's about having a pride in yourself and showing others the very best possible version of you.

Youth Employment UK identify three key self-management skills:
- Organisation
- Initiative
- Accountability

Firstly, you can't manage anything (let alone yourself) unless you are organised. You need to plan your time and the tasks that you need to complete. You will need to know which are the most important and the optimal order to complete them in. This might sound easy, but your list will be ever changing as new tasks are constantly added and you will need to be flexible to accommodate all the changes.

Another key part of self management is working on your own and not stopping to ask questions of your boss every ten minutes. No employer wants to sit on your shoulder all day making sure that you do your job. If they did – they may as well do it themselves and save the money they are paying you. Using your initiative – and trying to solve problems on your own is a great skill and one that will be greatly appreciated by your manager.

Finally, you have to be prepared to be accountable for the work you deliver. The ultimate responsibility might sit with your boss or line manager, but if you are the one 'producing the spreadsheet' or 'counting the bricks' you will need to make sure it is correct. Double checking everything before passing it on will not only ensure it is correct, it will demonstrate that you care about your job and that you care about the level of work you deliver.

Taking pride in your work will demonstrate a positive attitude and this will be welcomed by people in all aspects of your life. Being a go-to person to get a job done well is a tremendous skill to have and one that will serve you well throughout your life.

Self Belief

To get things done, you need to believe that you can do them. You need to be resilient when things get tough and stick at it. You need to learn from your mistakes, exude a positive attitude that will inspire others, and demonstrate that you are someone who is a 'doer'.

Youth Employment UK identify three key self belief skills:
- Motivation
- Resilience
- Positive attitude

Some people are motivated and some just can't be bothered. Quite often those who can't be bothered think that those who can "are lucky" or "have got it easy", but this isn't true. Anyone can get up early, do some exercise and then be ready to face whatever the world has planned for them – you just need to be motivated to do it. Being motivated to do something is much easier if you enjoy it and you can see the benefits. This is why the more you are in control of your own destiny (your education, your employment, your skills etc), the more you will be motivated to tackle life the best you can.

We all face setbacks or disappointments from time to time, the question is how long you are going to feel sorry for yourself and how quickly can you put them behind you and get over it. This is called resilience, and it is one of the key buzzwords that employers are looking for. If your performance drops at work even for a day, it can have a major impact on your team and the business as a whole. A resilient worker therefore is much more valued than one who isn't. Everyone makes mistakes from time to time – the key is learn from them, move on, and ensure they don't happen again.

Finally, as we discussed in 'self management' – having a positive attitude will ensure you have a positive self belief.

There is nothing worse than a 'Debbie Downer' who is constantly spreading negativity. A smile can go a long way – and no one ever failed to succeed by being too positive.

Why is the LifeLocation® Life Skills important?

The first thing employers will check is your qualifications, but evidence of your life skills will come a close second.

Life skills demonstrate to employers so much more than whether you can pass an exam. They want to know if you will be an active member of the team, they want to know whether you have potential to become a manager and they want to know how you will cope when things go wrong.

Life skills show them these things and more. They also show employers that you have the drive and determination to get them as they are usually gained through non-school or college activities like volunteering or work experience.

But they aren't just for impressing employers. Having a balanced set of life skills will aid you in your every day life from planning shopping lists to having the confidence to try new activities and visit new places.

Further Links

www.destination.org.uk - *Lots of specially commissioned and curated content relating to increasing your life skills*

Check your **local authority website** for lists of local courses and opportunities in your area

Barclays Life Skills
www.barclayslifeskills.com

National Citizen Service
www.ncsyes.co.uk

Duke of Edinburgh Awards
www.dofe.org

Go Think Big
www.gothinkbig.co.uk

Prince's Trust
www.princes-trust.org.uk

Youth Employment UK
www.youthemployment.org.uk

Outward Bound Trust
www.outwardbound.org.uk

Unstoppable Teen
www.unstoppableteen.com

Resetting your Life Skills

Soft or Factory Resets

- **Feel as though you don't have the required life and work skills?** – Don't worry most young adults think this. Start by focusing on the areas you feel that you are weakest in and look for opportunities to improve.
- **Worried that you are missing one or more of the essential life skills?** – Why not force yourself out of your comfort zone by doing something completely new like volunteering or joining a local club.

LifeLocation®
4. Networks

There is a phrase that 'older' people use a lot – usually when they have been turned down for a job or missed out on a potential opportunity: "It's not what you know, it's who you know!"

Essentially this means that people or companies help out their mates rather than offer the opportunity (fairly) to anyone who deserves it. The saying suggests that even if you are more qualified, or better suited than the other person, they will gain the opportunity because they are connected with the person offering the position.

It would be great to suggest that this is a myth, but it isn't. However, rather than feel sorry for yourself and feel the world is going to be against you; you will need to accept that it happens and make it work for you.

Many of the opportunities that are available for young adults never reach them. This is for a number of reasons:

> 1) Some organisations aren't very good at getting their message across, both in terms of making it look like it

is worth getting involved with and/or ensuring that it is seen by the right people

2) Some organisations don't have an unlimited advertising budget and therefore need to do things as cheaply as possible.

To provide an example – a company could easily spend £5,000 advertising a job vacancy (even a low level one). Instead, to save costs, a company might ask its networks if they know of any suitable candidates. This is a common occurrence and increasing numbers of positions are being filled in this way every day. This is why networks are important.

There are thousands of networks that you can join and you are probably already part of a number of them. A network is simply 'a group of people'. It could be your five-a-side Whatsapp group, your old school friends, or your extended family. You also have indirect networks, those groups that you are part of due to other people that you know. For example, your parent's work friends, your best friend's extended family or even your old teacher's college friends.

Within all these networks, there are people who know people who might have access to something you need. In the example of the company using its networks to recruit – if you know the right person (i.e. someone within the organisation's network) – you could be well on your way to getting a job interview for a role that hasn't been advertised.

Networks (particularly within a work and professional

capacity) are extremely useful. But to maximise them you are going to have to: a) know that they exist, b) know what they can provide you access to, and c) manage them so that when you need them – they are ready to give you what you want.

Managing your networks, doesn't mean that you have to be that annoying person that is always in everyone's faces asking if they have heard of any opportunities. However, equally, you cannot expect your old school friend that you haven't spoken to for a while to suddenly put in a good word for you with her boss – just because they are advertising a job that you fancy.

The trick is to find a sweet spot. A place where you are visible to your networks and easily reachable should an opportunity arise.

Your networks will constantly evolve, and new people will be constantly added whilst some will invariable drift away. This is important as the needs you will have from your networks will also be constantly changing.

This links back to the discussion about 'personal objectives' (see page 32). If you want to become a lawyer, then you need to join some networks around law. For example, you might join a LinkedIn group and from here make connections with local legal professionals. Likewise, you might search for the main legal companies in your area and follow them on social media. Even with a minimal amount of effort you will have already created a 'law network' and be significantly nearer to law opportunities than you previously were.

LinkedIn

LinkedIn is a social media platform for work people and it can be really useful in building useful networks and contacts for your professional life. It's a bit like Facebook for business.

On the site you can either make connections with other people or you can follow companies and organisations. Once you make a connection with an individual you can see their posts in your news feed and message them directly (and vice versa).

So if you are looking to get into a career in law, find out the companies that you'd like to work for and follow them on LinkedIn. This will then allow you to comment on their posts and learn about key personnel within the firm. Once you know who the people are you can request to become a connection to them.

There are lots of top tips to using LinkedIn but the main advantage is that it isn't massively used by young people starting out. This means that you might find that you can gain a significant advantage by setting up a profile and starting to build a network.

Multiple benefits of networks

Networks aren't just for finding a job – they can be used for work experience, or even getting onto your dream university course. Missed out due to one of your grades? Did you connect with the head lecturer on LinkedIn following the open day? Did you drop her an introductory note saying how much you were inspired by her talk and that it would be your dream to study on her course? It might sound a bit 'cheesy', but if there is only one spare place and two of you are wanting it - and the other person did do that – then maybe you might find yourself saying those famous words: 'it's not what you know but who you know".

Why is the LifeLocation® Networks important?

Creating networks and maintaining them are important for all aspects of life, whether it's to ensure you get a weekly exercise workout with your mates or creating potential opportunities for a job.

Starting networks from scratch is a difficult and time-consuming activity and for these reasons most people don't do it. This means that if you do it, you can steal a significant advantage over other teens and young adults who might be looking to take advantage of the same opportunities that you have your eye on.

Further Links

www.destination.org.uk - *Lots of specially commissioned and curated content relating to increasing your networks and connections*

Search for **local networking events** for lists of local events and opportunities in your area

LinkedIn
www.linkedin.com

Resetting your networks and connections

Soft and Factory Resets

- **Don't have any networks?** Firstly, you need to decide what networks you want to build. Write a list of all the people you know and then try thinking of the people or companies they are connected to that are connected to your area of interest.
- **Think about the organisations that you might want to connect to** - Are they on social media, do key people have a LinkedIn profile, can you volunteer there, what can you do to make them notice you?
- **Don't have a LinkedIn profile?** - Then why not register on the site and create one?

LifeLocation® 5. Money

As you progress into adulthood it is important to consider how much money you are going to need to enable you to do the things you enjoy?

Q. Why is money important?

Money is going to play a major part in your life. Regardless of how much you have, you will inevitability spend large periods of your life not having enough of it. Some people spend their entire life trying to get as much of it as possible. Does money make you happy? Probably not, but having just enough is always better than not enough.

You get money in two ways: 1) you earn it or 2) someone gives it to you. *You could add: 3) rob a bank - but this is going to take a lot of hard work to plan and execute – and it comes with a very high likelihood that you will get caught and put in prison. Plus, if you can plan a bank job you probably have most of the skills to get a regular job. So, it's probably best to stick with either 1 & 2.*

Earning it is pretty straight forward. You do a job and

someone pays you for it. The easier the job and the less skills or training that you need to do it - the less you will be paid. The harder the job (whether this is in terms of unsociable hours, the pressure you will be under, the responsibility you will have, or the amount of training you will need to do it), the more you will be paid. Therefore, a job involving filing or cleaning an office will be paid less than someone who has trained for a number of years such as a doctor, solicitor or an architect. In theory, more people can undertake the tasks of 'filing' or 'cleaning' than can perform heart surgery, so there will be a larger pool of people that employers can select from. Employers can pay less wages for positions where more people can do the job.

For someone starting out in their adult life - who wants a lifestyle that relies on a good salary - it would therefore make sense to pursue a career in a role that is more skilled and fewer people are able to do. This is not the only the way that you can earn a higher relative salary, but if you are low skilled it is going to be very difficult for you to get a job that pays a higher than average salary.

Q. How do I manage my money?

Before we worry about how much money we want to earn, let's start with managing the money we have now.

You will probably already have a bank account which provides you with some form of bank card that allows you to withdraw money or pay for things in shops or online. Often people only ever open one account and they keep it for life. With fewer bank branches open, online banking apps and widespread cash machines – it is unlikely that you have much to do with the company you bank with. As long as everything is working fine – happy days!

You can have a debit card from the age of 11 which means that when you pay for items with your card, the money is immediately withdrawn from your account – likewise if you make a withdrawal from a cash machine.

On many accounts you can also set up standing orders (a regular payment to another account/organisation) or direct debit (similar to the above but where the recipient requests a regular amount from your account). For most things like your rent, your phone contract etc you will pay via direct debit. You can usually choose the date that these payments go out of your account and most people choose dates that are a few days after their wage goes in. This means that regular bills are paid when there is the most money in the account. There is nothing worse than thinking you have money in your account before remembering that your car loan and rent hasn't gone out yet.

Monthly Budgeting

Having fixed regular payments enables you to keep a track of what you are spending.

Some people have a list (or a spreadsheet) that tells them how much they have to spend on a monthly basis after all the regular payments have gone out. This allows them to budget for the month and ensure that they don't spend more than they earn.

Being aged between 16 and 24 is a golden age and one that everyone in this age bracket should embrace. These are the years that will define the rest of your life – much more than your school years.

In reality you don't need a lot of money when you are younger. If you resist the temptation to 'want everything now' you will find life can be quite fun. If you want to emulate a celebrities Instagram feed then you are going to find life tough - but living within your means can still be great (and bear in mind your friends are probably all in the same boat).

Living a modest life now, means that you have the flexibility to get the skills now, to do a job in the future that you are going to enjoy and is going to pay you an income that will allow you to live the life you want to.

> *For some, this will mean having an income of over £100,000/year, whilst for others a more modest £25,000/year might be sufficient. The greater salary might mean a bigger house, newer cars, more glamorous holidays – but at the end of the day a house is a house, a car only gets you from A to B, and a holiday can be anywhere that gets you away from home for a while.*
>
> *A job with a salary of £100,000/year will probably involve longer hours, more stress and more time away*

from friends and family. There will always be someone in a bigger house, has a better car and better holidays – the secret is to find the point that you are happy with and aim for life at this level.

Using the years between your 16th and 24th birthdays to prepare yourself for being an adult will benefit you for years to come. For some this will mean going to university but it could equally mean working a basic job during the day and attending college on an evening. It doesn't matter how you do it – you just want to be in a position by the time you have reached Destination Adulthood where you are ready to be in control of your own life.

Resist the temptation to keep up with technology

Somewhere around 2004, Apple released the iPod – a device that played electronic music files. The original iPod didn't come with a wire that connected to a PC and it didn't play mp3's. In 2004, phones didn't connect to the internet and on-demand films meant ordering a DVD that arrived within 48 hours by post.

Now, 95% of 16-24 year olds have a computer in their pocket that is more powerful than the supercomputers of the past – but what has that got to do with your destination of adult responsibilities?

In 2022, a person born in 2004 will be 18. During their lifetime, they will have grown up with gadgets and consoles such as Nintendo Wii, Xbox, and Playstation, not to mention the full range of Apple and Samsung phones & tablets. For the first eighteen years of their life, they will have seen the continual introduction of new technology and lived in a disposable culture where obsolete technology is easily discarded in favour of upgrades of new and improved models.

Throughout this time, technology has become so critical to young adults that possessing the latest gadget has become an essential part of living. However, someone else has usually paid for it.

Maintaining the latest technology as a young adult is going to be difficult, as one of the biggest shifts from teenager to adult is going to come when you start to have responsibility for your mobile phone bill. With an average contract cost of £40/month plus the cost of the handset – you are looking at finding around £600-£700/year for the privilege of having the latest phone.

For such an essential part of living – this might seem a price worth paying – but on an average starting salary of £12,000/year – your mobile phone is going to be around 4% of your annual expenditure. This might be viewed as a small amount on its own – but as we'll discuss later, it's a big amount if you have run out of money a week before pay-day.

Of course, this assumes you are working. If you are at university – it's another cost to add to the student loan, but if you don't have a job (or if you only have part-time work) justifying the expense of the latest phone can be difficult.

Let's face it, technology is expensive and 95% of the things they do – you'll never need.

Only spend what you have

The key to 'money' is not spending more than you have. This might sound obvious, but once you hit 18, there are lots of people who are going to want to 'tempt' you to do this.

You will have spent your early teens being bombarded by people trying to sell you things. Traditionally companies have done this via adverts but now they heavily rely on clever subtle-advertising in the form of sneaky promotions via your favourite YouTubers and Instagramers:

> *"Hi, I keep getting asked how I keep my hair looking so great – well it's all down to @expensivehair – so why not give those guys a follow?" Or the other favourite "Hi, Just chilling on this paradise island thanks to @expensiveholidays drinking @expensivechampagne. #LifeGoals".*

As someone under 18 you might see these and think "I wish I could have that life… if only I had more money" but when you hit 18, you will find companies start to give you the ability to sample that life in the form of overdrafts, credit cards and loans.

It will start with your bank. At 18, the products that they can promote to you will change. The easiest product is an overdraft – an amount that the bank will let you dip into if your account balance goes below zero.

It may be that they don't even ask you. They might just send you a letter telling you that they have done you a massive favour and given you the flexibility of an overdraft – *what with them being really nice people right?* Well not quite. For a start they are going to charge you every time you use it and if you find yourself continually using it (which many, many people do) you are going to be paying for the privilege all the time.

This is how banks make profits – charging you for using their services. Having a salary paid in on the 25th and withdrawing it all on the 26th doesn't make them much money at all – but once you owe them money, they have you, and it can be very difficult to get out of it. This is what is known as the 'credit trap'.

Q. What is the 'Credit Trap'?

'Credit' is where a bank or 'somebody' agrees to lend you money on the grounds that you will pay the amount back over a set period of time (plus an extra amount – called interest). Credit comes in many forms (overdrafts, bank loans, pay day loans, credit cards) as does the amount of interest that you will pay for it.

Credit is not necessarily a bad thing. If you need a car for work (and you don't have savings) it makes sense to borrow the money at the beginning and pay for it over three or four years. By spreading the cost you are able to build it into your monthly budget – and whilst you are driving the car you won't begrudge making the payment. You might even get something back if you manage to sell the car after you've made all the payments.

Big items like a car (i.e. purchases that you will continue to use over the life of the loan) are ideal for credit and they help you to manage your money. It is the purchases that you make because you can't afford them, but you still think you need, that cause the real problems with credit.

At 18, if you are in work or at university the chances are that a bank will offer you a credit card. Banks are like all commercial organisations in that they are constantly looking for new customers. Winning you as a customer at 18, means that over the next 60 years you might pay in your salary every month into a bank account, take out a mortgage and borrow money for cars and home improvements. All these things earn the bank money – but they particularly make money from credit cards – especially from people who don't know how to use them.

Applying for a credit card is easy. Simply fill in a form, provide some ID and wait for the card to come through the post. At first you will probably only have small credit limit (say £500), but this is still £500 of free money that you can spend pretty much anywhere you like. *Except it isn't.* Every month the bank or credit card company will send you a statement. This is a list of all the items you have spent in the previous month (and possibly forgotten about). The round of drinks that you bought in the nightclub, the lunch you had with friends, those new shoes, or your weekly shop or filling your car with petrol. All of a sudden, you have a credit card bill for £500. If you can afford to pay it off, then great – you're winning and it isn't going to cost you anything. However, if you don't have the money then you are faced with the two-headed credit card monster – the 'minimum monthly payment' and the 'monthly interest charge' – and this how the credit card companies make their money.

If you can't or don't want to pay off the full amount, you can simply pay the most you can afford, as long as it meets the 'minimum monthly payment'. This might be around 2-3% of the total amount (so on £500 that's about £11/month). However, each month the credit card company will charge interest on the outstanding amount. This is called the APR and it's a bit complicated, but the higher the amount and the longer you don't pay it off – the more interest you are going to pay.

For example, you have £500 on your credit card, and the APR interest rate is 21.9%:
- If you were to pay back the minimum payment of £11/month (or 2.5% of the outstanding balance) it will take you 6 years and 9 month to repay, and the total amount of monthly added interest would be £403.
- If you pay back £25/month it will take you 2 years and 1 month to repay, and the total amount of monthly added interest would be £113.

- If you pay back £100/month it will take you 6 months to repay, and the total amount of monthly added interest would be £26.

But this isn't the end of it. If you maintain your monthly payments, the credit card company will start to view you as a good customer and offer you more credit. So, all of a sudden you have an increase in your credit limit and more 'free money' to spend. However, as the amount of money on your credit card increases so does the amount of interest you pay – and the amount of debt you start to have.

And this is how people start to get into financial trouble. If you have no money, and you feel in need of cheering up - you could put your purchases on a credit card. However you will only feel better for a short period of time and then the credit card bill arrives and it's back to needing cheering up again. There is no such thing as free money and getting into debt can be very difficult to get out of.

Managing your credit score

At some point you will probably want to borrow some money. This might be for a car or a mortgage to buy a house or flat.

Large (and expensive) purchases like this tend to be paid for by a loan rather than a credit card and as a result the interest rates are much lower. This is the reason that you wouldn't buy a house on a credit card!
The fact that the amount you are likely to be borrowing is

high means that more goes into vetting you to ensure you are a suitable person to have a loan. These checks include: how long you have lived in your current property?, your current income, your job status (full time, part time, zero hours contract?) and your credit score.

Your credit score gathers all the loans and credit that are in your name and gives a score on how 'trustworthy' you are with credit. Ironically, someone with a credit card debt that they are paying monthly will have a better credit score than someone who has never had any credit in their life. If you accumulated lots of debt and then failed to make any payments for a few months – your credit score will be low and this will likely prevent you from gaining additional credit. Lots of people use credit score checking such as landlords and phone companies and if you have a poor credit score your tenancy or application for a phone contract could be turned down.

Therefore, it is always beneficial to get onto the credit ladder – even if this is only to build up a good credit score. It is just that you need to ensure that you don't spend more than you can afford to.

Other sources of credit

Banks are not the only sources of credit. They tend to be the cheapest, but they also tend to be quite 'safe' (or low risk) in who they lend to. Other companies however, are prepared to take more risks – but for this they will charge significantly more interest and will be much more ruthless in ensuring that they get their money back.

Anyone walking through a town centre will have noticed the shops offering pay-day loans or seen adverts on TV or online for instant loans. These organisations will lend money but charge you a very large amount for doing so. They know that people who use these services are people who have been turned down from lower-interest loan options which means they are able to charge higher interest amounts.

Quite often, the loans are offered as short-term solutions to enable someone to get to pay-day. For example '£20 to borrow £100 for a week'. However, if the amount isn't repaid then they will continue to charge a high amount of interest until it is. It doesn't take long for a pay-day loan company to cause serious financial issues in your life.

What these organisations are doing is not illegal and in many cases they provide a valuable short-term financial solution. If you understand the terms of the agreement and repay the amount then they can work well, but if you fail to pay, then like banks they will charge you accordingly.

Another source of loan finance are 'loan sharks' – local 'companies' or individuals who also offer short-term loans at a high cost. However, whilst bigger companies will quickly deploy court action if you fail to meet your agreed payments, loan sharks might take a more 'direct' approach through violence or by taking your possessions as payment.

Q. Why is managing your budget important?

Life is tough, and it is even tougher if you can't afford to live at the level you want to. Using credit can allow a temporary trip to the luxury world of the rich and famous but if you can't afford to pay it back you could find yourself worse off and in a place where your only aspirations are putting food on the table and maintaining a roof over your head.

Think about it, everyone wants you to spend more money than you have. Those new boots might make you feel better for an evening, but are they worth still paying for three years later?

Everyone needs to manage their budget and needs to ensure that what they spend doesn't exceed what they earn. Yet, within this you also need to ensure that you have some slack for the unexpected things that invariably crop up in life to mess up your best made plans - your best friend's wedding, the exhaust blowing on your car, or the TV your mum gave you packing up halfway through a game of Call of Duty.

In order to manage your money you might find it beneficial to get into the habit of spending a couple of hours at the end of the month checking your bank statements and credit cards to see how much money you have spent and how much you have left. This can be an incredibly rewarding activity to do. At worst it will tell you that you spent too much and that you need to take it easy next month, but in the best case it might tell you that you spent less than you earned and that have some left over. This is when you can then start to make decisions on whether to buy a pair of new boots or save it for something else. Here you will realise that it is a lot harder to spend actual cash that you have saved than simply putting it on a card. It's quite unexplainable but when you are spending your savings, you really want to ensure that you get value for money compared to an impersonal transaction involving a credit card and someone else's money.

Understanding money (and the cost of money) is a great skill to have and one that will continue to be important throughout your life. As someone once said: "watch the pennies and the pounds will look after themselves".

Living within your means doesn't have to be boring. A night in with friends can be just as much fun as a night out and there are many activities that you can do that don't have to cost money. Dig out the old board games from your parents, (learn to) cook a big chilli and you have a fun evening that is a fraction of the cost. It's the same with days out. Go for a walk somewhere – get some fresh air – and you will be amazed at how much better you feel. Yes, you need a good blow out now and again – but just make sure it fits within your budget and that you aren't spending money that isn't yours.

Q. What are the costs of entertaining yourself?

Hey, guess what, once you are 18 – you can finally (legally) watch all those 18 films that you've been waiting to watch. All those old classics like 'The Exorcist' and 'The Godfather' that were made before your parents were born – *yeh right! No thanks!*

For most young people, media (TV, music, films, games, YouTube etc) is consumed in your bedroom, on your own. This means that one of the biggest changes in getting older (and getting your own place) is that your media will start to spread around the house.

This means that you will probably start watching a TV downstairs like a 'grown up' and that you might start to do it with other people. It is also going to start costing you money.

Q. What are the hidden costs of consuming your media in your own home?

When you are younger, you will probably be watching Netflix or listening to Spotify via a family account but what happens when you move out? Will you still have access to it? Will you keep one of the user accounts? What if the bill payer decides they don't want it any more – what happens then?

Streaming services aren't the only things you are going to have to pay for – if you move into your own place you are also going to need a TV licence.

The TV Licence

The TV licence is a strange thing. Running a TV network (like BBC, ITV or Netflix) costs millions of pounds every year. These organisations need to make content (programmes), which means paying actors, presenters, writers, directors and many other professional staff. They also need to broadcast it (either via an aerial, a satellite dish, or the internet) and they need to manage it – all of which is expensive to do.

TV networks recoup this cost in three ways. Some charge a monthly subscription fee (e.g. Netflix, Amazon Prime), some run advertising between and during programmes (ITV, Channel's 4 & 5), and some do a combination of the two (Sky). The BBC however is funded through a licence fee that it charges every TV-watching household in the country – regardless of whether viewers watch BBC or iPlayer programmes or not.

This amount is currently £150.50/year for a colour TV and if you don't pay it you can be fined or even put in prison.

Broadband & WIFI

As a rule, entertainment and fun things are going to cost you money.

Let's start with broadband. As a generation, the average 18 year old has spent their whole life with immediate (and free) access to a mythical thing that is only identified by the three bars at the top of your phone. Accessed via a secret code and delivered though a black box with a flashing light in the corner of the room, WIFI is the number one thing that most teens and young adults report that they couldn't do without.

And guess what – when you get your own place, broadband costs money too.

There are lots of broadband companies out there so you will need to shop around for the best deal. Don't sign up to the first company you find. You want the right one for you. If you do a lot of online gaming you are going to need a superfast connection, likewise if you are sharing your connection with a number of mates – *you will all want to ensure that you can watch the latest episode of your favourite streamed show at the same time without buffering* – you will need a fast connection. For the privilege of this you are probably going to pay around £30/month. If you don't need a superfast connection (i.e. you just want to use it for browsing the Internet) – you will find that you can get a cheaper service but this is probably still going to cost you £20/month. Prices will vary between companies so you will be able to shop around and compare deals to save money.

For instance, you might be able to get a deal with your phone supplier or your satellite/cable operator.

You will usually have to sign up for a minimum 12 months – which means that for the next year you will have to find around £240 just to have the ability to access the internet.

This means that just to watch Netflix on your own TV (in your own home) you will need to pay an annual cost of:
- *TV licence £150.50*
- *Subscription to Netflix (£7.99/month) £95.88*
- *Broadband contract £240*
- A total of £486.38

And it's even more if you want to add Spotify (£120/year), or Sky Movies & Sky Sports (an eye-watering £576/year).

Assuming you want Netflix, Spotify, and Sky Sports (including the TV Licence and Broadband) you are looking at around £1,200/year. If you also factor in a phone contract at £480/year (£40/month) you have an annual cost of £1,680 and this is before you have paid any rent, bought any food or spent any money on anything else like clothes, holidays, or going out and having fun.

To put this into context, if you earn the minimum salary for an Apprenticeship you will receive £7,605/year. If you have a job that pays minimum wage you will receive between £11,992 (18-20-year olds - £6.15/hour) and £16,009 (25's and over - £8.21/hour) *This is based on working 37.5 hours/week at April 2019 figures.*

DESTINATION ADULTHOOD | 125

If you work less hours (i.e. you are on a zero-hours contract) you will obviously earn less, but sadly your home entertainment costs won't decrease similarly.

Why is the LifeLocation® Money important?

Money plays a vital role in life and so it is essential that you plan a destination that mirrors the amount of money that you want.

Some people want lots of it, whilst others are happy with just enough. Whatever your destination, money will dictate where you work, how much pressure you are under and the number of hours you will be expected to put in.

But earning money is only one aspect. Once you have it you need to ensure that you manage it effectively and budgeting on a monthly basis is a good habit to adopt.

Further Links

www.destination.org.uk - *Lots of specially commissioned and curated content relating to managing your money*

Money Saving Expert
www.moneysavingexpert.com

Two useful budget planners:
Prince's Trust
www.princes-trust.org.uk

Citizens Advice
www.citizensadvice.org.uk

Resetting the amount of money you have

Soft and Factory Resets

- **Not managing your money?** Take some time to set up a spreadsheet or find a notepad and make a list of all the monthly outgoings you have. Add them all up and take away this amount from your monthly income. Look ahead to the coming month and work out how much money you either have left or that you are planning to spend. This will tell you whether you can afford a new purchase or whether you need to cancel one of those big night outs.
- **Is your monthly expenditure higher than your monthly income even when you have cut all the fun things out?** If you are at this stage then you might need to consider a more serious life change. Either earn more money (through a new job or a second part-time job) or go through all your monthly expenditure and look at ways you could reduce it (walk to work, use a different supermarket, downsize your accommodation etc) or a combination of all three.

- **Are you in a credit trap that you don't feel as though you can get out of?** Go along to Citizens Advice (there is one in most towns) and they will help you by going through all your debt and coming up with a solution that will make it easier for you.
- **Are you spending more on entertainment than you can afford?** Believe it or not people used to exist without Spotify and Netflix. Why not just switch it all off, and read a few more books or re-watch a few of those DVDs that are on your shelf? Failing that, there's always YouTube. Remember there is lots of free entertainment out there if you look for it

LifeLocation®
6. Health & Wellbeing

It is important that if you are going to enjoy and maximise your Destination Adulthood, you need to be in the best physical condition possible. Obviously not everyone is starting from the same position. We all have a unique set of circumstances that prevent us from maximising our potential as a superhero.

These circumstances are different for everyone. It might be a disability, it might be a debilitating illness, or might be mental health challenges. It might even be a combination of all three.

Throughout this book we have discussed the importance of taking responsibility for your own Destination Adulthood and that everyone will have their own particular destination and journey to reach it. When planning for this it goes without saying that in some cases, certain people will face barriers and challenges that are beyond their ability to change. Health and wellbeing issues would fall under this area.

However, everyone has a choice of how they deal with

these issues and has the opportunity to set the best possible destination within the parameters of their unique situation.

As a person who fortunately has an average level of physical and mental health, I cannot even begin to imagine the daily challenges that those below average health face. I have however spoken to many young people who would class themselves in this bracket and my experience is that the greater the challenges faced, the more pragmatic and optimistic the person tends to be.

The old adage is that: "there is always someone worse off than yourself", and if someone with serious diagnosed problems can manage to look positively at life then perhaps that is an inspiration for all of us.

Smoking, Alcohol and Drugs

You don't need this book to know that these things aren't great for you. If you have one or more of them as part of your lifestyle then at some point it is potentially going to hold you back.

Everyone who gets involved with them starts by saying they won't become a major part of their life, but before you know it they move from 'just to be sociable with my mates' to 'just to take the edge off the day' to being an every day activity.

There are lots of reasons to avoid these particular

destinations but mainly it's because they won't do your mental & physical health and wellbeing any good and they are going to take a significant amount of your money.

Q. How can I start taking control of my own health & wellbeing?

Around 10% of the population are born or acquire a condition that minimises their ability to manage their health more positively. Everyone is different and seeking to define a single solution for a large diverse and disparate group is almost impossible.

Hopefully those who are living with a life-debilitating condition are receiving the support that they need. However, many young people do not perceive that they need support or need to change their lifestyle.

Navigating everything that life throws at you is difficult and if you are to do it with any degree of success you need to have the best health and wellbeing you possibly can.

As a teen or young adult you think you can eat, drink, smoke and ingest anything you want. This is because you think you are going to live forever.

As a young adult, you are physically stronger to fight illnesses and your metabolism will allow you to have more than just the occasional fast food burger. However, that ability doesn't last forever and before you know it, you get out of breath quicker, you need a larger size in clothes, and you are much more susceptible to getting colds and aches. Welcome to adulthood!

Your physical health is one thing that you can manage, but it is much harder to control your mental health and wellbeing.

People have suffered with poor mental health for years. The difference is that now it is being diagnosed and that people are starting to talk about their conditions. No one can truly understand what another person is going through in respect to their mental health. You can take great pride in showing a bruise from a sporting injury and everyone will understand how much it hurt and when it has healed. You don't have this luxury with mental health – it has no direct visual signs.

I have made a conscious decision to not provide advice around mental health in this book other than to say that if you feel that you (or one of your friends) needs support in managing it, you need to visit a doctor/GP or encourage your friend(s) to do so.

Everyone is different and everyone has a different ability level of coping.

> *From a personal point of view, I would recommend healthy eating and lots of exercise. However because I'm not a professional health expert or have undertaken a diagnosis of everyone who reads this book, it would be remiss of me to prescribe it as a blanket solution. What is good for one person is not necessarily good for someone else.*

Mental health is a undoubtedly a ticking time-bomb and it is an area that is going to need lots of funding, support and understanding to get the issue under control. This essentially means that a consistent, nationwide support service won't be immediately forthcoming. This is why you need to take responsibility for your own health and wellbeing and ensure that you do everything possible to be the best version of yourself.

Health starts with regular exercise

Public Health England (PHE) - the organisation responsible for protecting and improving the nation's health and wellbeing - recommends that every adult should take part in "at least 150 minutes (2½ hours) of moderate intensity physical activity each week, in bouts of ten minutes or more."

'Moderate intensity physical activity' is defined as any activity that causes you to get warmer (sweat a bit), breathe harder and get your heart to beat faster. This means that 'brisk walking' is fine, but the Friday night pub crawl sadly isn't.

PHE are not a group of masochistic teachers trying to make you do PE in the rain. They are a collection of experts, providing advice to ensure you live the very best possible life that you can.

Getting into the habit of exercising regularly is not just about avoiding becoming overweight or obese – although it will help do this. Exercise is going to help things inside your body as well as how it is seen externally.

Being healthy will reduce the likelihood that you will suffer a stroke or heart disease – and it can also help prevent and manage a number of long-term illnesses and conditions. Imagine planning your ideal Destination Adulthood only to be not well enough to enjoy it.

Q. Is being healthy that important?

Not everyone has the choice of being healthy. Many people face health challenges that they have lived with from birth or that they acquire at a young age. However, the vast majority do have a choice and as a young adult you are at your peak potential to be fit, active and healthy. Whether or not you decide to be is a decision that you alone will choose to make.

One of the key benefits that teens and young adults have in their life is 'time'. As you get older, this available time will slip away from you. There are lots of things on the horizon that are going to eat up your time – a new job might involve a longer commute and/or starting a family (however far away that might seem) will almost certainly take away some of your free time and result in you being less active. In addition to being 'more inactive' there is also a risk you will start to eat unhealthily and spend even more time sat down or being 'sedentary' as the health boffins call it.

And so, starts the exercise (or non-excising) vicious circle. You don't have time, so you don't exercise, which makes you feel lazy, which makes you more likely to not exercise. This then becomes a habit, which means you fill this time with other non-exercising activities, which means you don't have time (and we are back to the beginning). One of the hardest parts of exercising is breaking the circle.

But first let's look at the reasons not to exercise:
1) You don't need to
2) You don't have time
3) You can't afford it
4) You already do enough

1) You don't need to

Your body might be able to burn off all your calorie intake as a teen, but it starts getting harder as you get older. As those extra pounds start to add up they become a lot harder to get rid of.

Ask most people over the age of 40 if they can still get in the jeans they wore as an 18 year old and most will laugh (or cry) in your face. Even those old folk inappropriately dressed in Lycra, running or cycling around your neighbourhood, are probably several notches further on their belt than they used to be.

Most use their big birthdays '30', '40', '50' as the year they will get in shape by, but these come and go, and before you know it, you are buying clothes a couple of sizes up, thinking about comfort and dressing like your parents. Over half of the adults in the UK are classed as overweight or obese. If you find yourself in this bracket then you risk your quality of life diminishing. Ensuring that you are fit and healthy in your twenties will prepare you for your thirties and beyond. For every year you don't address it, it will just get harder to get back to where you are now, and you will have to expend twice the energy trying.

2) You don't have time

We all live 24 hours a day and very few of us spend hours on end bored, wondering how we can fill our spare time between college, our job or our other commitments. Some of us like to stay in bed as long as possible, some of us like to play computer games, and some of us are happy ploughing through all the box sets on Netflix.

If we are being honest, for most people not having the time is just an excuse for "I can't be bothered." This is where the vicious circle starts. Not being bothered is a symptom of not exercising. If you exercise, you feel more positive, optimistic and bothered about things. Having a positive outlook will ensure that you get much more done – and it will start with you finding time in your life to exercise.

3) You can't afford it

If you feel as though you can't exercise because you can't afford a gym membership, then think again. A 30-minute brisk walk around the block isn't going to cost you anything.

Plus, doing this instead of going to the gym has just saved you the transport time of getting there and back – winner!

If money is tight why not search YouTube for an exercise work out? Grab your shorts and your trainers and turn your bedroom into you own private gym. If you want to add weights - simply use tins of beans or something similar!

4) You already do enough

When asked, very few people describe themselves as 'inactive'. After all, walking for the bus or to your mate's house is being active – right? No. In a recent survey that was undertaken with over 1000 young people, 39% of teens and 48% of young adults (aged 18-25) said they exercised for less than one hour a week yet most still described themselves as 'active'.

This means that large number of young adults don't do enough exercise and this number is only going to increase as people get older.

Diet

As well as exercising – it's also important that you eat well. This doesn't mean fine steaks, lobster and caviar, it means having a balanced diet that contains all the main food types. There are five main food groups: Carbohydrates (pasta, rice, oats, potatoes, etc), Protein (meat, fish, eggs, vegetable protein, beans etc), Diary (milk, cheese, yoghurt etc), Fruit &

Vegetables and Fats & Sugars. Most dieticians recommend that you should eat a balanced diet which combines elements from each food group.

Of course, some people are allergic to certain foods & groups, and some people choose not to eat certain foods based on their religion or their personal preferences.

It is not the aim of this book to advise on specific diets, other than to say that the more that you can build a diet that works for you and incorporates as many food groups as possible, the better chance you will have of eating "healthily"

Like exercising, when you are younger you can eat what you want without too many repercussions. Living on a diet of takeaways for a week whilst your parents are away won't do you too much harm, but when the week becomes a month, and the month settles into all the time – then you are going to start feeling and noticing the effects.

Many of the arguments for not eating healthily are the same for not exercising – you don't need to, you don't have time, you can't afford it, you already do enough. Add to this 'you don't know how to' and you have a full set of excuses that is going to make you a 'Deliveroo' or 'Just Eat' prime customer.

Eating fresh is usually better than eating processed (i.e. eating food prepared in a factory). The main reason is that you will know exactly what ingredients are in your meal. Many processed meals use lots of salt and sugar and preservatives to ensure the product has a long shelf life.

On their own, none of these are a problem, however if you have a sweet tooth and like fizzy drinks, the sugar in your meal might push you over your daily recommended amount without you even realising.

Maybe it's time to learn to cook

Everyone should be able to cook a few meals – and that doesn't include toast!

Cooking your own meals will not only be healthier than a similar meal available in supermarket but it will also be significantly cheaper.

With the internet at your fingertips it has never been easier to find a recipe and a step-by-step video cooking demonstration on YouTube.

Why not try to make mince (either meat-based or plant-based) your best friend as it's a cheap, flexible food and you can easily turn it into a shepherds' pie, a lasagne or a chilli-con-carne. 15 minutes preparation and 30 minutes cooking time and you'll have a nutritious and healthy meal. The more you make it, the better it willl get and before you know it, you'll be wooing a partner with it by candlelight. Add to this a spicy chicken pasta (or a protein-based substitute), a curry and a Sunday roast and you'll be almost self-sufficient. Either complement it with a couple of ready meals or some more adventurous home-cooking and you'll be sorted for the week.

Cooking for yourself will also save you money and time. In many cases, you can make enough for a number of meals. A big pot of chilli will enable you to either put it in the fridge for the day after or freeze a number of portions to eat in the following weeks.

Finding time to cook is like everything – if it isn't currently in your daily routine, it's hard to see how it fits. But the beauty of cooking is that it doesn't have to an isolated activity. You can do it watching the TV, or listening to music or a podcast. You can even do whilst Facetiming your mates.

Q. What about Sex Education?

Again, this is an area that is beyond the remit of this book other than to say you probably shouldn't be Facetiming you mates whilst doing it.

As a young adult, society has never been as open about sex and there has never been as many sources available to get advice on how to do it safely. However, if you are worried (or embarrassed) about something it can be very difficult to find the confidence to ask for help.

It can also be difficult to search for advice online. If people are taught anything about the internet it's not to type 'Sex' into a web browser.

The main thing to remember is that whatever you want to know – someone else has probably already asked that question. If you want a good place to start why not look at Sexwise (sexwise.fpa.org.uk) or @sxwise on Twitter. They have a very no-nonsense, straight-forward approach about everything related to sex – from contraception to STIs to pregnancy (either avoiding or planning) all the way through to sexual wellbeing. Sexwise are part of the sexual health charity FPA -so they know their stuff!

Maximising your physical and mental health is essential as you aim to reach your Destination Adulthood. The journey is going to be tough and you are going to need all your strength to complete it. And once that destination is in sight, the last thing you want is for your health to prevent you from enjoying it.

You should also keep an eye on your friends and family too. Whilst the stigma of talking about personal problems is reducing, some people are still unable to discuss challenges that they are privately living with. If you suspect someone is struggling you might want to discuss the issue with a professional on their behalf who will be able to advise you on the best course of action.

Why is the LifeLocation® Health & Wellbeing important?

The last thing you want after many years of planning and hard work is to arrive at your Destination Adulthood and not be in a good physical or mental condition to enjoy it.

To ensure you have good health and wellbeing you need to look after yourself by exercising regularly and eating healthily. Of course you can deviate from time to time, but if you avoid turning treats and occasional laziness into habits, then you will be well on your way to your ideal Destination Adulthood.

Further Links

www.destination.org.uk - *Lots of specially commissioned and curated content relating to maximising your physical & mental health and wellbeing*

Search your **local authority website** for lists of local services, events and support in your area

The NHS
www.nhs.uk

Health for Teens
www.healthforteens.co.uk

Childline
www.childline.org.uk

Young Minds
www.youngminds.org.uk

Papyrus – prevention of young suicide
www.papyrus-uk.org

Kooth (not national support but useful information)
www.kooth.com

Alcoholics Anonymous
www.alcoholics-anonymous.org.uk

Smokefree National Helpline
www.nhs.uk

Talk To Frank
www.talktofrank.com

Sexwise
www.sexwise.fpa.org.uk

B-eat Eating Disorders Youthline
www.b-eat.co.uk

The Mix
www.themix.org.uk

National Gambling Helpline
www.BeGambleAware.org

Resetting your health & wellbeing

Soft and Factory Resets

- **In need of help?** Firstly you can't wait for someone else to fix you or hope that a problem will just sort itself out.

- **Do you feel as though you have an issue?** If you have a physical or mental health problem it is essential that you visit a GP as they are the best equipped to make you better.
- **Worried? Embarrassed?** If you are worried or embarrassed about attending a surgery – don't. They deal with much more embarrassing problems every day and they are trained to deal with them – this is their job.
- **It's your responsibility to get better** Remember, whist a doctor may give you a prescription to help you get better – it is also important that you take responsibility for your own health and wellbeing by living a healthy lifestyle. You will benefit your life by exercising more and eating healthily – find the time to do it and you'll even find that it saves you money.

LifeLocation® 7. Housing

Q. How do I put a roof over my head?

Since the beginning of time people have needed a roof over their head. Whether it's a cave or a penthouse apartment – there is "nothing quite like home" – and at some point in your life, you will want your own place.

The majority of people live in their family home until they go to university or earn enough from working to allow them to move out.

Moving away from the family home is a really big deal. Many will trial it whilst they are away at university, but most will still expect the sanctuary of their bedroom to remain untouched for the full duration of their course. After all, you want to be the one that makes the decision on moving out. No one wants to come home to find that a parent has converted their room into a home gym or craft room.

Studying away from home will mean living in either official on-site student accommodation or a self-found student house off-campus. In both instances you will discover a new-found freedom and acquire a whole new set of responsibilities including cooking for yourself and learning how to use a washing machine.

Going home for the weekend or holidays will be great at the start when you are being looked after and spoilt, but you will soon start to miss your independence. This is the point that you will realise that you don't ever want to move back home.

Of course, most people only make the decision about moving out when they have a job that enables them to do so. However, some people need to move out when life presents difficult problems.

Having your own place means lots of increased financial outgoings - council tax, utility bills (gas, electricity and water), household insurance - but the biggest cost is undoubtedly the cost of the property you will be living in.

This section will look at all the housing options that are available and how you go about making the transition from the home you grew up in to getting your own place.

Q. What are my housing options?

If you want your own home, you essentially have three options:
- Buy a property
- Rent a property via a private landlord
- Rent a property via a social landlord

Buying a property

The average price of a house in the UK was £150,000 in 2018. However, because this is the average price, you will find the cost in some areas is cheaper whilst in some it is significantly higher.

To buy a property you don't need to walk into an estate agents and pay the full amount. You can, but the majority of people don't – mainly because most people don't have that amount of money.

There are three main costs to buying a property:
1) The mortgage
2) The deposit
3) The hidden costs

1) The mortgage

Most people buy a property using a mortgage. A mortgage is a loan provided by a financial institution such as a bank or building society. Like the loans discussed in Money, in exchange for giving you a mortgage, they will charge you interest. Most mortgages tend to be over a long period of time (such as 25 years) and you pay the loan and interest back monthly over the full term of the agreement. Whilst the interest rate might seem low (typically around 4%), the way it is calculated and the amount of time you will take to pay it back means that if you were to borrow £150,000 it would cost you about £1,000/month and you will pay the original amount plus about another £130,000 in interest. A total repayment of £280,000.

This might seem a large amount – but you soon forget about the interest and the time you have left to pay. You simply just get used to paying the monthly amount.

Help to buy

If you are looking to buy a new-build house i.e. a brand new house on a new housing estate, you might find a number of special offers and incentives.

Under a Help-to-buy scheme, rather than buy a house outright you purchase a share of the property (between 25%-75%) and then pay a small monthly rent on the remaining balance. Then, when your circumstances change and you are in a better financial situation, you can purchase the remaining share of the property.

Many house builders and social housing organisations (see page 154) offer Help-to-buy loans which are run by the Government.

> *Please note this scheme may not run indefinitely and it is highly likely to change in the future. You can find out more and keep up to date at www.helptobuy.gov.uk*

You might also find that house builders can offer further incentives such as reductions in solicitor and valuer costs and some may even offer to pay the stamp duty (see page 151) so it is worth fully exploring this option.

Buying with someone else

It makes sense to split the cost of such a big purchase decision, and buying with a friend (a boyfriend, girlfriend or just a friend) can significantly reduce the cost that you pay. This might become more necessary in areas where £150,000 isn't the average house cost - such as in major cities or desirable areas.

Obviously, you need to be good friends as the last thing you want is for the relationship to break down and one of you wanting to move out (and wanting the money they have put into the property handing back). However, suggesting that two friends will fall out sooner than a couple who have made a formal commitment is a naïve notion and as a result this method of house buying is rapidly growing in popularity.

2) The deposit

If you want to borrow £150,000 from the bank, they will want to know that you can be trusted with it. The last thing they want is for you to get a mortgage and not pay the money back. If you stop paying the amount back, the bank will take legal action against you, evict you from the house and sell it to recoup the money. This all costs the bank money, so to ensure that they don't end up out of pocket they build in some financial security. This financial security is the deposit that you contribute and ensures that the bank don't take all the risk and fund your purchase 100%.

Most banks are happy with a deposit of 5% of the purchase

price, however if they feel that you are slightly more high-risk (perhaps you've moved around a lot, lived in lots of different houses, you have a low credit rating (see Money), you haven't been in your job for very long, or you are self- employed and don't have a fixed monthly income, they may ask for more.

This might not seem fair, but at the end of the day they don't have to lend you the money. It is your responsibility to convince the bank to trust you. If they are in any doubt about lending you the money– they will simply refuse and turn down your mortgage application.

A 5% deposit on a property selling for £150,000 is £7,500. This means that you will need to be able to contribute this amount in order to get a mortgage for the remaining 95% (£142,500). This is usually the main obstacle to buying a house as finding a deposit can be really difficult – particularly if you don't have savings, don't have much money left at the end of the month or don't have wealthy parents!

Of course, the good news is that your monthly payments and the amount of interest will be less on £142,500 compared to £150,000 (a saving of around £125/month and around £10,000 in interest over the term of the mortgage), though you won't appreciate this when you are looking down the back of the sofa for spare change.

3) The hidden costs

Sadly, it doesn't stop there. You will also need to appoint a solicitor to handle the purchase which could cost you up to

£1,000 and you will need to pay a valuer to visit the property to ensure the property is worth the amount you are going to pay and it isn't going to fall down the minute you move in.

Oh, and if you buy a property between £125,001 - £250,000 you will need to pay 2% stamp duty to the Government (another £3,000 on that £150,000 property). *That amount actually goes up to 5% on properties over £250,001!*

So that £150,000 property is going to cost you £11,800 before you move in. (£7,500 deposit, £1,000 solicitor costs, £300 for a valuer and £3,000 stamp duty) This is before you have even made a monthly payment or bought any furniture!

Fortunately there are other ways that you can put a roof above your head.

Rent a property via a private landlord

Once most people have realised that buying a property is really expensive, they quickly start to look at renting. Essentially it means that you get to live in a house (or flat) that someone else owns. Monthly payments will be roughly the same as a mortgage payment (perhaps a little higher) but obviously once you have paid it – it's gone. Some people refer to renting as 'dead money' because you are paying for something that you will never own. However, with the high price (and limited availability) of housing, renting can be the best option of having your 'own' property.

If you want to rent a property it isn't quite as simple as walking into a letting agent and getting the keys. Firstly, you will have to complete a 'letting form' which will include all your personal details including a space for references. Like the mortgage application, the person who owns the property wants to make sure that you are a reputable person, are not going to wreck the property and are not going to miss any of the monthly payments. Within the letting form you will be expected to provide evidence that you are in employment and that you can be trusted. The latter can be evidenced by supplying details of previous landlords but if you are renting for the first time, you obviously won't have this.

It is likely that the details that you supply will be credit checked. This means they enter all the information into a computer programme and it provides an answer of whether you are trusted are not. If you fail the test, you are back to square one, if you pass you can advance to the next stage.

Properties are usually made available for a fixed period of time (in blocks of six months - usually 12 or 24 months). Once the duration is agreed, a contract will be formed which will protect you and ensure that you have the guarantee of a roof over your head – i.e. the landlord can't evict you just because they feel like it. This is not to say that your tenancy cannot be extended beyond this, but this is something you will discuss as your tenancy comes towards the end. If you want to remain in the property, are a good tenant, and the landlord is happy – you will find that renewing is a straight-forward process.

However, before you get the keys, you will need to pay a bond (a kind of deposit) – which is usually one month's rent.

This amount protects the landlord from you 'doing a runner' or damaging the property. Unlike the deposit on a mortgage, you will get this amount back when you complete your tenancy, assuming you have made all your payments and they are happy with the state you left the property in.

Once you get the keys, and you pay the monthly rent, you won't need to worry about anything until you come towards the end of the tenancy. At this point you will have a conversation with your landlord (or letting agent) and discuss how you both want to proceed. If everyone is happy you can simply extend the tenancy, or if either of you are not happy, or your circumstances have changed, the tenancy will simply end and (assuming you have left the property in a good state) your bond will be returned to you.

Rent a property via a social landlord

Within the UK are a number of social housing organisations that exist to provide disadvantaged people (such as non or low waged individuals) with the opportunity of having a property to live in.

Obviously not everyone has the ability to buy a property or the credit history to rent via a private landlord. Social housing used to be provided by local authorities (it used to be called 'council housing') but over the last twenty years the housing, political and financial landscapes have changed and as a result lots of smaller organisations have been set up to provide affordable social housing.

Throughout the country there is a lack of social housing. With demand outstripping supply – it will come as no surprise that it is the most in need that are housed first.

Social housing still needs to be paid for. If you have a wage you can pay the rent yourself, but if you are low waged or unemployed, the rent can be paid for from benefits (i.e. Universal Credit).

Unfortunately for young people, the benefits system is not in your favour. The government won't pay any housing benefit until you are over 24. This means it is very difficult to get access to social housing until you reach this age.

There are exceptions – but support from social housing usually comes in the form of 'essential' and 'last-ditch' rather than facilitating a lifestyle choice. So, if you are single parent or you are escaping an abusive relationship you will find yourself at the top of the list and above someone who is struggling to rent because they have a bad reference due to not looking after their last property.

Iif you are looking for a particular type of property in a specific area this might not be for you. The small number of available properties means that you can't afford to be fussy. For most people utilising the support of social housing, the priority is a secure location with a roof over their head rather than the location and type of property. With social housing you get what you need. You don't get an extra bedroom to have in case your friends visit, and nor will you necessarily get a garden or somewhere to park. If you are lucky enough to get a room with a view it is likely that it is on the ninth floor of a tower block with no guarantee that the lift will always be working.

Q. How do I find a property?

Probably the best place to start is with an online search of estate agents, letting agents and housing organisations. Save them all in a file in your browser and start to get a feel of how much a property is going to cost. This will vary significantly between the type of property and where it is located. Once you have spent a bit of time doing this you will soon know where you can (and can't) afford to live. If you can't afford anywhere locally then you might need to consider somewhere further away.

Why is the LifeLocation® Housing important?

It's a brilliant feeling when you finally leave home and get your own home. Whether it's a small flat or a giant mansion, nothing can beat unlocking the door with your own keys.

The cost of doing this means that it is getting harder and harder to do, but with some proper planning (and a bit of saving up) it can be achievable.

Admittedly your first home might not be 'exactly' want you want (size, area, neighbourhood), but it will allow you to develop as a person without having the parental pressures and ensure you are one step closer to your Destination Adulthood.

Further Links

www.destination.org.uk - *Lots of specially commissioned and curated content relating to housing*

Search your **local authority website** for lists of local housing organisations

Buying a house or renting

Rightmove
www.rightmove.co.uk

Zoopla
www.zoopla.co.uk

Help to Buy
www.helptobuy.gov.uk

Homeless issues

Centrepoint
centrepoint.org.uk

Resetting your housing options

Soft and Factory Resets

- **Happy living in the family home but worried that if you move out you will lose some of your home comforts?** You have to move out at some point. Perhaps if money is tight you could consider sharing with a friend to reduce the expense?
- **Are you living somewhere that is unsustainable?** Are you living on a friend's couch, in an unfriendly family home or sharing with an unsuitable house-mate? If you need your own place contact your local housing association as they may be able to help.
- **Are you living in a property that you cannot afford and are struggling to pay the rent or mortgage for?** It is important that you contact the landlord or bank before it gets too late. In many cases they may well look to help you.

LifeLocation®
8. Where You Live

Often the biggest challenge is getting out of the comfort zone of family life and taking the first steps on your own.

For many years, young people have stayed in the area that they were born, but now the fragmented jobs market and economic uncertainty means that more and more young adults are faced with the choice of staying local and getting a 'regular' job or having to move away from the family home in order to maximise their potential.

Whilst this might seem like a big scary decision, in reality with improved communication and transport links, living at the other end of the country can seem like living just a few miles away.

Whilst you are making your decisions about your Destination Adulthood, the place where you live will be very important.

Q. Does it matter where I live?

Believe it or not, where you live is really important. Without knowing it, your very being – from your head to your toes – has been influenced by the surroundings you have encountered growing up.

Someone living in a busy cosmopolitan city will have a very different outlook to someone who has grown up in a rural area – and this is going to be a fundamental factor in how you define your Destination Adulthood and your journey to reach it.

But where you live is much more than just a place on a map. It will affect the amount of money you can earn, the number & variety of jobs that you can apply for, the proportion of your wage you will have to spend on rent, the variety of culture available to you and your likelihood of finding true love. Where you live is important.

To demonstrate this - let's split things into two halves: Where you live now and where you might live in the future.

Where you live now

The UK is a fantastically diverse country that offers a variety of different areas to grow up in. London is one of the most visited cities in the world and within its centre offers a multitude of job opportunities and ways to spend an idle afternoon. Sport, art and theatre are in abundance – as are some of the finest museums in the world (many of which are free to enter) – all within easy reach for the 12 million London residents.

Compare this with the highlands of Scotland, the marshlands of Norfolk, or the industrial areas of the North of England or South Wales, and you have a fragmented country offering different levels of opportunities for young people.

It is very rare for families to move between areas. Many families have three or four generations who have always lived within a 2-mile radius. Historically people stayed local because they had a lifetime of friends, memories and ample opportunities for employment. However, this is changing. Jobs are no longer in plentiful supply and we are no longer in a pre-technology age where visiting someone at their house is the only way to keep in touch.

Where you grew up will have a strong influence on your outlook. If you have grown up in a city, you might find it difficult to believe that someone your own age has never left their town. Likewise, if you have grown up in a rural area you might be surprised to discover than large numbers of people have never seen sheep in the wild.

This is obviously going to be a factor in your aspirations and the knowledge that you have in considering your unique Destination Adulthood.

As a rule, if you live in an affluent area you will have a more positive outlook, whereas if you live in a poorer area you will have a less-positive outlook on life.

This isn't always the case but over the years – and after

running many focus groups with young people from all parts of the country – it is really noticeable how the location of a person's home can affect their personal development.

For example, a group of Year 11 students in a school with a relatively affluent catchment area will be a year more developed and mature than a group of Year 11's in a less affluent area. This development will be demonstrated in many ways: academic ability, levels of concentration, confidence in speaking within a group, listening and understanding questions. These are basic skills that appear to be determined by the place that you live.

This means that if you are from a less-affluent area, then you are going to have to work slightly harder to catch up with someone who is from a more affluent area. This isn't something that you can change immediately, but it might mean that you only feel confident going to university when you are 21 rather than when you are 18.

This isn't something to look negatively at, quite the opposite. Realising you aren't ready to make a big decision at 18 but could be at 21, might save you lots of money. It is pointless going to university just for the sake of it. By waiting a couple of years you might have refined your Destination Adulthood and have a much clearer idea of what you want to do and have the extra skills to achieve it.

But as we keep saying throughout this book – there is 'then' and there is 'now'. There is 'before you have read this book' and there is 'after you have read it'. What has happened is done – you can't do anything about that. What you can do is take responsibility for your future and seek to tweak the areas of your life that need improving.

Just because you have grown up in a certain geographical area doesn't mean that you have to spend the rest of your life living there. Limiting where you live will limit the choices that are available to you.

Where you might live in the future

Packing your possessions into a bag and moving away is undoubtedly a big deal.

For many, the start of this process is going to university in a different town. Picking the location is as important as picking the course – and it provides the opportunity to match a town or city to your personality or future aspirations.

Since the Further and Higher Education Act was passed in 1992, the number of universities has significantly grown and there is now a place to study in most towns and cities in the country. You want to live in a city – you've got it! You want to study somewhere picturesque and historic – you can do that too!

For the purposes of this book we will split geography into the two extremes of 'city' and 'rural'. Yes, that it is a big scale – but with 6.3 million 16-24 year olds in the UK, it is impossible to cover the unique characteristics of everybody's neighbourhood in the country.

The extremes are used to illustrate the points made. Some people will live in inner city tower blocks, some in areas that are on the outskirts of cities, some will live in towns that are half-urban/half-rural and some will live in areas where all they can see is fields and hills. By picturing your location and imagining where in the scale you fit – you should gain an idea of the pro's and con's of your location.

Living in a city

Cities are a great place to be when you are young and independent, however unless you already live there, it comes at a cost as they are really expensive places to live.

It will certainly impress your friends though, and as soon as you have a place to live they will be dropping hints for an invitation, it's just a shame that you might not have enough money to go out and do it justice when they come to visit.

It's unlikely that you will be able to afford to live right in the centre of the city – so you might find yourself living in one of the smaller conurbations (i.e. mini towns and villages) around the edge. The 'cooler' the area (i.e. the places with the best bars and restaurants, good transport links etc), the more expensive it will be. You will probably find that most younger people will live in the 'edgy chic' area - an upcoming area that will have cool urban bars but will also have certain areas that are best avoided after dark!

On the plus side – this is as bad as it gets, and it is a rite of passage that lots of people go through. The abundance of jobs and opportunities means that if you work hard you will soon be able to progress and as this means an increase in salary, you will have more money available to either go out with, put towards a bigger flat, or get one nearer to the centre.

Growing up in a city gives you a different outlook to those living in other areas. If you live in an inner-city area – you will have invariably had to develop street wise skills and you will be much more likely to be exposed to crime than someone in a rural area like the North of Scotland. Without knowing it, you have already developed a number of valuable life skills that can be used in other ways. Just developing the skills to forward plan a safe route home – makes you a trainee project manager, and that mental toughness and confidence is the backbone of skills needed within sales.

Living in a rural area

The biggest advantage of living in a rural area is also, for many, its biggest negative – it's quieter and the pace of living is much, much slower.

The fact that there are fewer people means that there are less jobs available as organisations are obviously reluctant to set up businesses in locations where there isn't an abundance of skilled labour. This problem is doubled by the fact that many traditional industries that previously drew its labour from these areas are disappearing which means that rural unemployment is a real problem.

This is not to say that jobs and opportunities don't exist - it's just that they are more limited. However, if the Destination Adulthood that you want is obtainable within a rural area,then great. You just need to consider the destination that you want and ensure that the location that you choose to live can deliver it.

Why is the LifeLocation® Where You Live important?

The UK is a massively diverse country with each part of it having very unique features.

Just because you have lived in one area all your life doesn't mean that you have to live there forever. Technology and transportation means that you can easily keep in touch from wherever you are.

As part of your Destination Adulthood, you will need to live in a place that provides the employment and activities necessary. For some this will mean living in or close to a big city whilst for others it will mean being based in a more rural location.

Further Links

www.destination.org.uk - *Lots of specially commissioned and curated content relating to where you live*

Search your own and other **local authority websites** for lists of local employment statistics and information

Resetting where you live

Soft and Factory Resets

- **Is where you live holding you back?** Why not draw up a short list of where you think you would rather live. Perhaps you could go and visit these places to see if they are right for you
- **Are the opportunities available that you require in order to reach your Destination Adulthood?** If they aren't, you may need to consider a more appropriate place to live
- **Remember to consider the housing options** in the Housing section as accommodation prices will vary significantly between areas

LifeLocation®
9. Family & Friends

"You can choose your friends but you can't choose your family", "blood is thicker than water", "You can't live with them, but you can't live without them." Etc etc etc.

Families define your personality, your aspirations and your outlook on life.

> *Perhaps a family member, friend or loved-one bought you this book? That probably means they want you to succeed and make the most of your life.*

The only thing all of us have in common is that somewhere in our past it took the coming together of a male and a female to create us. From that point onwards, we all embark on a unique journey influenced by millions of variables.

Living in the early part of the twenty-first century the question of 'what is a family?' could generate a book in itself.

Needless to say, 'family and friends' comes without a pre-defined definition. Family doesn't necessarily mean blood relatives, and friends don't need to pass a 'BFF' test. Family and friends are really important as we transition into adulthood.

As well as providing us with access to important networks (see Networks), they also provide us with essential support both physically and emotionally.

Life is really difficult if you try to navigate it solo. At times everyone feels as though they are alone, but this should be occasionally rather than all the time.

This is not about measuring your friends by the number of 'likes' your last social media post got; this is about having 'real people' who will drop everything to see you when you need a shoulder to cry on, or will turn up with a smile (even if they don't feel like it) when you have something to celebrate.

Not everyone has the luxury of an abundance of friends and the support of a loving family.

Maintaining family relationships and friends (like everything) can be hard work and takes a certain amount of effort. However, when both are functioning well you will find your life enriched – whether it's through the joy of a communal Sunday lunch or the creation of shared memories. Doing things with other people exposes you to different ideas and opinions and makes you a more rounded individual.

As you approach adulthood it is important to ensure that you do everything in your power to maintain the relationships in your life. This will not always be easy. Your friends will sometimes do something that you disagree with or a family member might say something that makes your blood boil. Equally you could say or do something that they don't like, and this will prompt them to get out their voodoo doll of you.

When relationships do get strained you have a choice. Do you walk away (often the easiest option), grit your teeth and let it go (a difficult option) or apologise for your actions if you are in the wrong (by far the hardest option)?

Learning the skill of 'making up' is one of the most under-rated skills you can possess. The word 'sorry' might only have five letters and two syllables, but it is word that lots of people cannot find the strength to say. This is not the variation of 'sorry' that comes with a shrug and a general air of 'I don't really mean it'. This is the 'pit of your stomach' 'sorry' that you are saying because a future relationship depends on it. These are the moments that define friendships and ensure that you both grow old together.

It's easy to lose touch with people especially if you move away for work or to a university, and more so when you start to develop new friendship groups. Sometimes all it takes is for one of you to send a quick text to see that things are okay. Remember, they might look as though everything is okay on social media, but nothing beats a personal text to show you want to keep in touch. It might only take a second to send, but the warm fuzzy feeling it generates lasts significantly longer.

Why is the LifeLocation® Friends & Family important?

Families & friends define our personalities, aspirations and our outlook on life.

So why are friends and family important? Quite simply because life is so much easier when its enjoyable and family and friends provide the soundtrack to a lifetime of laughter and fun.

Maintaining friendships and relationships with your family is not always straight-forward, but where possible you should try as hard as possible to do so.

Not everyone has the luxury of family and friends, which is why you have to do everything in your power to keep what you have.

Further Links

www.destination.org.uk - *Lots of specially commissioned and curated content relating to friends and family*

Search your **local authority websites** for lists of local events and mediation services

Childline
www.childline.org.uk

BBC Advice
www.bbc.co.uk

Barnardos
www.barnardos.org.uk

Relate
www.relate.org.uk

Missing People Helpline
www.missingpeople.org.uk

NSPCC
www.nspcc.org.uk

Resetting your relationships with friends & family

Soft and Factory Resets

- **Have you lost touch with a family member(s) due to a disagreement in the past?** Is this something that could be repaired? Why don't you make the first move to reconnect?
- **Not seen a friend in a while?** Why not drop them a text and arrange to meet up?

LifeLocation® 10. Community & Democracy

Q. Why is community & democracy important?

With a UK population of 67 million, it is easy to think that you are small, powerless and inconsequential. Why should you bother getting involved in politics when you can't change anything and it doesn't really affect you.

This couldn't be more wrong.

Politics affects everything. The number of police in your area and how quickly they might respond if you call 999. The time it takes for the local A&E department to look at your sprained ankle that you damaged playing sport. The amount of tax that the Government take from your monthly pay, or the amount of Universal Credit that you might receive if you are unable to work due to a disability. Every day, decisions are being made that effect many aspects of your daily life. You have a choice as to whether you want to influence these decisions or simply say *"nah - can't be bothered – it's nothing to do with me"*.

The word 'democracy' comes from Ancient Greek (them again) and it derived from the words 'demo' meaning 'people' and 'Kratia' which means rule. This shows how long the concept of 'people' being involved in decision and 'rule' making has been around.

Yes, democracy and politics are a bit complicated – but no more difficult than learning to drive or teaching a parent how to use Snapchat!

Q. Can you give me a quick introduction to British politics?

Throughout the UK, there are 650 Members of Parliament (MPs) who each represent an area of the country called a constituency. Each MP is responsible for representing the interests of the people who live in their constituencies (or 'constituents' as they are known as).

So wherever you live, you will have an MP that is paid to represent *you*. If you have an issue that is not being dealt with by official channels (such as an issue at the local hospital, with your benefits or with your tax) you can make an appointment at one of the regular MP surgeries (meetings), raise it with them and ask them to help you out.

Unlike most people in jobs – you actually get to decide how well they are doing by voting for them (or not voting for them) at a General Election (or a bi-election) every five years or when one is called by the Prime Minister. Therefore, if you feel your MP is doing a good job – vote for them, or if you think someone else could do better – vote for someone else.

This is complicated slightly by the fact that MPs also represent specific political parties. As well as representing the interests of local constituents, they also come together with other MPs of the same party to try and run the country.

MPs come together in the Houses of Parliament. With 650 MPs each representing a political party – the party with the most MPs form the government and get to run the country.

Running the country, means that one of them gets to be the Prime Minister, whilst other MPs get to be in charge of Government departments like Treasury (tax and money), Health (running the NHS and keeping people healthy), Home Office (looking after the safety and general running of the country such as managing the police, prisons and immigration), Education (being in charge of all the schools), Work & Pensions (largely in charge of benefits), and Business. In total there are about 20 top positions, and these make up 'The Cabinet'.

Different political parties tend to have different ways of running the country. Some believe that you should pay more tax so that more money can be given in benefits to people that need it, whilst other parties believe that if you tax people less, they will have more money in their pocket which they will spend and therefore create more jobs. Some believe that we should restrict the number of immigrants coming into the country whilst others believe that immigration is essential to fill certain jobs that UK citizens are either unqualified for or don't want to do.

How you feel about these issues, combined with how you feel about your current MP will define who you vote for in an election.

Q. Should I vote?

Having a vote is a right that every British, Irish or qualifying Commonwealth citizen resident at an address in the UK has when they reach the age of 18 (unless you are in prison). To ensure you get to vote you have to be registered – which means filling in a form online confirming your name, age and address.

At the last General Election (in 2017) only 65% of the population that was eligible to vote did so. This means that 35% (around 17 million people) didn't vote. To put this into context, this would easily be enough to change the final result. These numbers are similar for every election – and shows that everyone's vote is important.

Some people say that they don't vote because it is 'fixed'. This couldn't be more wrong. If you want proof, volunteer as a vote counter on election night and spend several hours collating each and every vote. These volunteers work extremely hard and their every move is scrutinised and double checked. Furthermore if the result is close – they count every one of them again (and again, if necessary!) This is done in each of the 650 constituencies. Whilst you might be able to argue that there is plenty wrong with our political process – the integrity of the vote counting is not one of them.

The actual act of voting is quite simple. During an election, within every constituency, there will be lots of small 'Polling Stations' situated throughout the area. These could be in schools, community centres or even the local sports hall. If you are registered to vote, about a month before the date of the election you will receive a voting card telling you where to vote. On the day you can visit the location between 8am-10pm. When you enter the voting room you will be asked to confirm your name and address, they will cross you off their list (so you can't vote twice) and you will be given a piece of paper (a voting slip) with all the local candidates printed on it. You will go into a private booth and you simply put a cross in the box at the side of the person you want to vote for. Once you have done this you place your voting slip in the slot of a sealed box. This box is only opened by a vote counter (in a central location) after all votes have been made and the 10pm deadline has passed.

It can be a bit nervy when you do it for the first time – but it is really easy and you get a great feeling that you have done something really important and powerful. Lots of people in history have fought (and died) to ensure that everyone has a vote – so your small act of voting is an easy task considering.

It is particularly important for young adults to vote. Whilst MPs and politicians represent their constituents, they are largely concerned with those people that vote for them. If the majority of people who vote are older, then it will be their issues that they are largely focused on. If a significant proportion of the voting population are over 50, then it will be issues around pensions and care homes that they primarily deal with. However, if large numbers of young people vote then they will be forced to look at the issues facing this age group – Apprenticeships, zero-hours contracts, university fees – and do something about it.

As one person you can't change the world, but you can make a start. You can research the issues, read the leaflets that come through the door, talk to friends and family and try to understand what sort of country you want to live in.

Whilst feeling detached from the wheeling and dealing in Westminster is understandable, there is also a type of politics that takes place much nearer to home.

As well as electing MPs, you also have the power to elect local councillors. Every town and city in the UK has a local council and like national Government they make important decisions that will affect you at a local level. These types of issues include how often your bins are emptied, whether or not to build and run facilities like leisure centres and how much council tax you should pay. Whilst local councils employ people to work within them (council officers), these people are overseen by local councillors who are elected by residents.

If MPs represent large areas (like whole towns), Councillors represent smaller areas like villages (or wards). Like MPs, they represent the interests of residents and businesses within their local area and then they all come together to make the big decisions affecting that Council. They are also similar to MPs in that they also represent political parties. The party that is most represented by councillors is said to be 'in power' and it will usually represent consistent views with the national party.

Councillors are voted in (or out) more often than MPs and you will have the opportunity to vote every two years (usually in May). The process is exactly the same as voting for MPs. You receive a card, visit the polling station, place a tick in the box of the person you want to vote for and place it in a sealed box.

Quite often local elections coincide with general elections which means that you could find yourself voting for both an MP and a local councillor at the same time – though it would be on separate voting slips.

Again, it's easy to not vote – but getting involved means that you start to understand some of the issues of your community and how elected officials plan to resolve them.

In the run up to an election, your letterbox will be bombarded with information of individuals that want you to vote for them. This will usually take the form of a leaflet and will show photographs of them standing in front of various local landmarks making grand statements of how they have (or intend to) improve your area. If you are lucky, they will also pay your house a visit and make themselves available for a chat.

> *The conversation could go something like this:*
>
> *Candidate: Hello, I'm [insert name] and I'm a candidate for this area. Are you intending to vote?*
>
> *At this point they are hoping for a yes/no/go away – but it is also an opportunity for you to say: "I don't know yet. How are you planning to help young adults in the next two years?"*
>
> *From their response you should be able to gain an idea of whether you want to vote for them.*
>
> *And this is democracy in a nutshell – you have one vote (the same as everyone else) and it's entirely up to you to choose who to give it to. If everyone thinks that their vote is worthless then it will be, but if everyone makes the trip to the polling station – then it will become powerful and you will start to influence decision making in your area.*

Q. Can you explain political parties to me?

If it was as simple as voting for people that you liked, it would be a much easier task. Unfortunately, party politics play an important part in democracy and people tend to vote for a political party rather than the person.

Traditionally in the UK we have two main parties – Conservatives and Labour, though a number of smaller parties have strong presences in provincial areas (Scottish National Party in Scotland, Plaid Cymru in Wales and Democratic Unionist Party in Northern Ireland), and some other parties have a handful of MPs such as the Liberal Democrats and the Green Party.

As was said previously, each party stands for a set of principles. These can be researched online or by reading material produced by them.

Most people tend to keep their political views private. The reason that the polling station has individual booths for you to enter when you make your choice is that it is no one else's business who you vote for. Everyone is equal, everyone has one vote and your vote is your choice. Whether you have a politics degree or you don't know your MP from the PM, it doesn't matter.

Of course, some people don't like this. They want you to vote for the party that represents their views and in some instances they might become overpowering. This might be a friend or family member – but just because they make the case for their choice doesn't mean it has to be your choice.

Keep it a secret, tell the truth, lie or tell the world - it's up to you. The most important thing is that you vote.

Why is the LifeLocation® Community & Democracy important?

Your role as a British citizen is just as important as anyone else's and it is important that you exercise your democratic right to shape the country that you live in.

As well as voting in elections it is also important that you look at opportunities in your life to benefit the local community that you live in.

It's easy to cut yourself adrift and not get involved, but if everyone did this the country (and our local communities) would be in a much worse state.

Being an active member of your community will give you an increased sense of purpose and you will be able to carry this feeling of positivity into other aspects of your life.

Further Links

www.destination.org.uk - *Lots of specially commissioned and curated content relating to community and democracy*

Search your **local authority website** for lists of local events and opportunities to get involved with local community activity

Register to vote
www.gov.uk/register-to-vote

UKYouth
www.ukyouth.org

UK Parliament
www.parliament.uk

Find out who is your MP
www.parliament.uk/mps-lords-and-offices/mps/

Find out who are your local councillors
www.gov.uk/find-your-local-councillors

Find out how your MP voted on various issues
www.theyworkforyou.com

Care for the Environment

Young Peoples Trust For The Environment
www.ypte.org.uk

The Wildlife Trusts
www.wildlifetrusts.org

United Nations Climate Change
www.unfccc.int

Resetting your role in local democracy

Soft and Factory Resets

- **Not registered to vote?** Do it today. Visit your local authority website and follow the relevant links.
- **Not sure about who to vote for?** Read their websites and see if any of them are saying things you agree with. Start to read newspapers online and watch TV news to build up a picture of what is happening in the world, what needs to be fixed and how UK politicians are proposing that they do it.
- **At a local level – what are the key issues that need to be sorted in your area?** Could you be the one to do something about them?

TRANSPORT

LifeLocation®
11. Transport

The closer you get to your Destination Adulthood, it's less likely you are going to want to grab that upstairs back seat on the bus. For one, you'll start to notice that a bunch of 'younger people' are always in them and secondly, you might start to find the bus a bit restrictive.

Buses, trams and public transport are the mainstay of any teen and young adult's life journey, but as you get older you start to need to be in specific places at specific times. You don't want to arrive at your destination wet because it was raining and the last thing you want is to get chewing gum on your best outfit before a night out. Yes, buses are great, but they are a bit '*limited*!'

Q. I would like my own transport, what are my options?

You have four main options:
1) The car
2) A moped
3) A bicycle
4) Walking

1) The Car

Before you can drive a car, you will need to have passed your driving test.

Learning to drive

The driving test is in two stages – the 'theory' test and the 'practical driving' test.

The driving theory test has two parts. Part one is a multiple-choice test made up of 50 questions (of which you must score 43 or more to pass). Part two is a driving hazard detection test where you must identify potential hazards as you proceed along a virtual road.

The practical driving test involves about 40 minutes of driving that is supervised by a driving examiner and a number of other tests including how good your eyesight is, vehicle safety questions, general driving ability, reversing and independent safe driving.

Before you take your test, most people have driving lessons either provided through a driving school or by family/friends (or a combination of the two). The advantage of going with a qualified driving instructor or driving school is that this is what they do for a living. They will provide a vehicle and because they have hours and hours of experience, they are able to teach you how to drive. It will likely cost you about £25/hour-lesson but there are usually deals available and the price might decrease depending on the number of lessons you book. This is what driving instructors do for a job; they have to have an official qualification and they will have taught hundreds of young adults how to drive. Plus the cars they use to teach you have dual controls – so if you forget to brake, they won't!

Going with a family member or a friend is obviously cheaper, but you have to be aware that it can take your relationship to breaking point (and often beyond it). It is usually the case that the person giving the lesson is the owner of the car, and therefore their primary objective is not to teach you to drive, but to ensure that you keep the vehicle in one piece and don't damage it. Remember they don't have dual controls!

This means that every extra 'rev' you give the car, every missed gear 'crunch', every time you get too close to another vehicle, they are going to tense up and occasionally (or regularly - depending on their levels of personal calmness) raise their voice. Under normal circumstances you might be able to handle this, but you may be equally tense, and you may occasionally (or regularly - depending on *your* level of personal calmness) raise your voice back. This will usually occur when you have stalled in the middle of a busy roundabout with a bus heading towards you!

Passing your driving test and getting a driving licence is another rite of passage that most people navigate through on their route to be becoming an adult. Unfortunately, getting the piece of paper is a lot of stress for nothing unless you have access to something to drive.

Access to a car

Most people start driving by being placed on their parent's insurance policy and are given the keys to a family car.

Whether you get the keys or not will largely depend on the car(s) your family own. If the one car you have access to is a big, super powerful 4x4 family car, then it is going to be expensive to insure you, which will probably mean that you can't sack off the bus too soon. If your family own a smaller car then you might find that it is financially viable to add you to the policy. You could offer to pay the difference yourself, but let's face it, if they don't ask you to contribute – there is no point in offering!

Borrowing a car will be fine in the short-term but you will soon get fed up of having to ask all the time, plus, if anything happens to that car (whether it was your fault or not), you are getting the blame. Borrowing a car is great, but once you get a taste for driving, you will soon want a car of your own.

Getting your own car

The holy grail of driving is having your own car. However, this is going to be really expensive. In the Money section we looked at how much you need to earn to live on, and owning your own car is going to put another significant dent in your finances.

The four main costs of a car are:
- The purchase price of the vehicle
- Insurance
- Petrol
- Unpredictable running costs

When you start to think about owning a car, you will need to set your expectations at a level where you are not going to be disappointed. Cars are expensive – not just when you buy them, but when you insure them, fill them with fuel, pay your annual road tax and try to fix them when they go wrong.

As a rule of thumb, the smaller, the older and the less powerful car that you buy, the cheaper it will be.

Insurance is all about risk. The lower the risk you are, the lower the chance the insurance company feel you will have an accident and the less likelihood they'll feel they have to pay out to repair your vehicle. If you are young, are an inexperienced driver and have a super fast sports car – the chances are you will be more likely to have accident than a 65-year old in a Honda Jazz who has been driving for 45 years and never had an accident. This is why you might be paying £3,000/year for insurance and the 65-year old is paying £300/year.

The longer you drive without an accident, the cheaper your insurance will become. Each year you go without putting in a claim gives you a 'no claims bonus (NCB)'. The more NCB you have, the lower your insurance will be. But you only start to earn NCB when the policy is in your name. If you are simply added to a parent's policy then they qualify for the NCB not you.

There is a quick way to tell how costly your insurance is going to be. Every vehicle has an insurance group. Small, less powerful cars are low numbers and the 'rally cars' have high numbers. Unless you (or your parents) have money to burn, you should probably be looking for a vehicle in a single-digit insurance class.

Remember you are at the start of your adult life and there is lots of time for you to get your dream car. Regardless of the type of vehicle you have – you will always look fondly on your first car. This is the vehicle that you are going to share some important life moments in. It will take you on dates, it will go on holiday with you, and you'll probably clean it more than your bedding. It will become one of your best mates and in years to come you will be nostalgic for the old, rusty, slow, unreliable piece of metal that is your first car. Whether it's a Porsche or a Skoda – you will remember its registration number all your life. You never forget your first!

Buying New or Old?

So you have rejected all the cars that you can't afford and the ones that you wouldn't be seen dead in – and this leaves you with a list (which is probably a short list!) Now it's time to go and buy it.

The best thing to do is grab someone that knows about

these things (parent, friend, work colleague) and go and visit some garages and get a feel for what they are like in the flesh and how much it is going to cost you. Before you do this, it is a good idea to know what your budget is. You will either need a lump sum if you are going to buy the vehicle outright or a deposit and an idea of the monthly amount you can afford if you are going to get a loan.

Once you get on the garage forecourt – the car salesman is going to want to sell you a car and s/he is going to do all they can to persuade you that 'this is the one!' This is after all, what they do as a job – and many are very good at doing it.

This is why it's useful to have as much information as possible before you start looking. If you know the amount and the insurance group that you can afford, then you will be able to assess whether the available cars are good value or not. Don't rely on the price that is displayed in the window – this is merely the starting point and could be significantly reduced if you are ready to do a deal straight away. Likewise, if you do find a car that is a perfect match for you – you don't want to lose it because you have to go away and work out if you can afford it.

So new car or old car? This is ultimately going to depend on your budget. Buying new means that it is likely to be more reliable but buying old means that it will be cheaper.

Buying new has a number of advantages. The vehicle will come with a warranty which means that if anything goes wrong the garage will fix it without any cost to you. A new car also means that you can choose the colour, only you has driven it, and it will smell nice when you collect it. New cars also don't need an MOT (see page 192) and if you are really loaded you can specify a range of additional extras like a panoramic sunroof, satellite navigation, Bluetooth connection to your phone or bigger alloy wheels.

Garages and dealerships will also have flexible ways for you to pay for it.

However, many people never ever get to buy a brand-new car. Whilst they are undoubtedly expensive, something else happens that puts people off. They instantly lose their value due to something called 'depreciation'. Say you went to buy a brand new £12,000 car in a showroom, the minute you picked it up and drove it away it would instantly be worth less money – perhaps as much as 20%. In the minute that you drove it out of the garage, put some music on and checked yourself in the rear-view mirror, your car could have lost around £2,000 in value. Of course, you don't see this because you will probably have the car for three or four years and by the time you come to sell it you would expect it to be worth less money. But the reality is that it is worth significantly less almost immediately. This is because you bought something new and if someone else bought it, it would be second hand and less desirable.

Sometimes you can pick up a nearly-new car (perhaps the garage used it for test drives), but these tend to be rare and are quickly snapped up.

It is more likely that you will be looking for a car that is 'second-hand' – i.e. it has had one (or more) previous owners. Often people tend to own cars for around three to four years and as a result there are lots of cars available around this age.

They will however differ in price. A car that has done low mileage or has been kept in an immaculate condition will be more expensive than a car that has been driven into the ground and not looked after. The key to buying a second-hand car is not what it looks like, but what condition it is in mechanically. At three to four years old, cars tend to 'go wrong' and things start to break. What you find very quickly is that it can be very expensive to fix a car. Tyres that need replacing? £60/each. A new exhaust? £150. Replacement brakes? £200. Some second-hand cars may still have warranty on them, which means you will have some peace of mind – but as a car owner you are always only one puncture away from having to cancel your weekend because you are skint.

It's not as though you can just pretend that there isn't a loud knocking noise coming from the engine. If your car is over 3 years old, every year it has to have an MOT. This is an annual test that you have to pay £30 for; where a qualified mechanic looks at your car to ensure it is safe to drive on the road. In actual fact what happens is you pay a mechanic to tell you everything that is wrong with your car and how much it is going to cost before you are allowed to take it back on to the road. If you can remember that feeling of dread waiting for your examination results, well multiply that by 100 as you brace yourself to be told how much of the money you don't have, you are going to have to find to get your car back. This is the point that you start to remember bus travel fondly. Oh, and if you are thinking that you'll just avoid having a MOT – that's illegal and you can't renew your insurance without one.

Previous generations grew up with family members that liked nothing better than putting on a pair of overalls, lifting up the bonnet and hitting bits of metal with a spanner. But now all cars (even the cheaper ones) are so full of technology that it's almost impossible to fix mechanical problems unless you work part time on a Formula 1 team.

Being a car owner (like so many other things as an adult) is expensive. However, unlike other purchases, it continues to cost you money every time you use it (and even if you don't). On the plus side though, owning your own car will give you a tremendous level of freedom and allow you to go wherever you want, whenever you want to go.

2) A moped

> *"And I'm like, honestly, I don't know nothing about Mopeds. He said I got the one for you, follow me."*

Macklemore might have travelled 'Downtown' on his moped, but for any young adult they are a great way to get about and significantly cheaper than buying a car. Okay, it's not as glamorous as a car, you'll get wet when it rains, and they aren't ideal for romantic first dates, but when A-to-B is only a couple of miles, you'll get there quicker on two wheels than you would have via the eight wheels of the bus.

Costs will vary significantly depending on the type of moped or scooter that you buy but you could easily purchase one for around £1,000. Then with road tax, insurance and a moped licence you would be looking to get on the road for around £1,500. You will still need to fill it with petrol, but you should expect to get twice the miles per litre of fuel than you would get from a car. And, as you would only be making short journeys (they aren't really designed for long distance commutes) you would find that even if you did 100 miles/month that would only cost you about £10/month in petrol.

If you add to this that you can easily store it in a garage (or your hallway), you don't have to get stuck in rush hour traffic and with the right outfit you can look quite cool on it – you have a great little mode of transport. You will have to take a separate driving test – but this is significantly less involved than a driving test for a car. Bike driving tests are designed around age and the bike you want to drive. They combine compulsory basic training (CBT), a theory test and a practical test. A licence for driving a low powered scooter on your own, differs from a licence for a powerful bike and to carry passengers on the back.

Let's not kid ourselves that they are the safest mode of transport. It's only going to take a little knock or an unseen pothole and you will be travelling sideways horizontally; and if you aren't wearing full motorcycle leathers (which the chances are you won't be) then it's going to take a little while for the skin to regrow on your arms and legs.

However, whenever you are on your moped you are going to be conscious of the dangers and as a result you would be expected to have 100% concentration on the road. Whereas in a car, there are lots of potential distractions: changing a song, playing with the 'sat nav', turning the heater on, eating a snack or even just chatting with a passenger. Accidents happen with any vehicle – it's just that the risk of injury is greater as a result of a moped accident.

3) Riding a bicycle

It's slow, it's hard work when you need to go up a hill, and you arrive at your destination hot and sweaty. On the flip side though, it keeps you fit and active and it's cheap.

Using a bicycle to get around is great if you live in an area that is relatively flat and has designated cycle paths, but again, they aren't great for dates. If you've ever ridden a bicycle on a main road – in rush hour traffic – you will also know how dangerous it can feel.

This mode of transport is probably not great for every journey, but if you only work a few miles from home, and you have a route that can avoid main roads – you could find that cycling to work and back saves you a large amount of money. It will also possibly save you having to pay for a gym membership too!

You can pick up a bicycle for around £100 (possibly

even cheaper if you buy second-hand) and if you aren't particularly mechanically minded you can pay around £30 for a full service. Here a bicycle mechanic will strip everything down and return it to you in perfect (and safe) working order.

You might find that some employers have cycle-to-work programmes. As part of these they may even pay for a brand-new bicycle for you – or at the very least subsidise part of its cost.

In recent years lots of bicycle repair social enterprises have set up. These are local charity-based organisations who repair old unwanted bikes and sell them on. Within these groups they also often offer maintenance classes (so you can learn to repair your own bike), and some even offer road safety lessons. These organisations are worth checking out as it can be an even cheaper way of getting an instant method of transport.

4) Walking

Finally, the cheapest method of all – walking. Admittedly not everyone has this ability, but for those that do it can severely reduce the strain on your finances.

One of the first things that happens when you get your own transport is that many people stop walking. At least when you use public transport you walk (or occasionally run) from your house to the bus stop, or from the bus stop to your final destination. The minute you get a car – that distance is shortened from your destination to wherever you park.

Short distances can be easily eaten up by walking. The average person walks at 4 miles/hour. This means that in thirty minutes you should be able to walk around 2 miles. Factor in rush-hour traffic and there might not be a great difference in which is the quickest travel option.

Walking home is a great way to unwind from the stresses of the day. Exercising creates endorphins which is a chemical in the brain that creates positivity. Having a break between work and home, where you are active, where you are able to switch off and where you can let your brain create positive chemicals – is great for both your physical and mental health.

You obviously need to plan your route in advance and make sure that you are safe at all times. During the winter months, when the mornings and evenings are darker it is best to avoid quiet, unlit areas. However, if you stick to busy areas (main roads etc) walking can be a very satisfying way of getting about.

Why is the LifeLocation® Transport important?

Travelling on public transport is something that everyone has done, but it's a great feeling when you are finally able to ditch the bus pass.

Whilst most people inevitably gravitate towards owning their own car it is worth remembering that cycling and walking can be great complimentary ways to get around (especially for small distances) and they don't harm the planet!

Further Links

www.destination.org.uk - *Lots of specially commissioned and curated content relating to transport*

Search your **local authority website** for lists of local transport information

Book your driving test
www.gov.uk/book-driving-test

Book your theory test
www.gov.uk/book-theory-test

The Highway Code
www.gov.uk/guidance/the-highway-code

Find driving schools, lessons and instructors
www.gov.uk/find-driving-schools-and-lessons

Find driving lessons

BSM
www.bsm.co.uk

The AA
www.theaa.com/driving-school

Red Driving School
www.reddrivingschool.com

Resetting your transport options

Soft and Factory Resets

- **Is the bus starting to become a pain?** Have you been putting off taking your driving test or are you happy to take lifts from friends and family? Why not arrange some lessons and start the process.
- **Can't afford a car?** Why not look at other modes of transport that are significantly cheaper

LifeLocation® 12. Travelling

TRAVELLING

Travelling and visiting somewhere different is good for your soul – it opens your horizons and it takes you away from your daily routine. On holiday, without your parents, means you can be who you want to be. You can let your hair down, you can dress up and can indulge your passions in the things that you really enjoy. Everyone should go somewhere different from time to time – it's good for you.

Your first holiday without your parents, is the first time many young adults get to experience proper freedom. This means not having a curfew, no one watching how many drinks are consumed or anyone to check how many of your five-a-day you have eaten.

Your first holiday with friends is another rite of passage that signals the move from teenager to young adult. It's also going to be an experience that you will remember for all of your life.

The location is largely irrelevant. Whether you are camping in a field in the rain (likely), sleeping three to a room without air-con in a dodgy hotel in Kavos (possibly) or chilling on the back of a yacht in the Mediterranean (unlikely) – it's the people that will make it, rather than where you actually are.

For many, the dream is a boozy resort in the sun, full of other young adults all looking for the same great time. No parents, no restrictions, #nofilter. However, there are just as many that feel that this is their worst nightmare - like spending your holiday back at school with the people you couldn't wait to get away from.

This is the beauty of a holiday – you can go anywhere you like. It's like a Subway sandwich - choose the bits that you like and create your own. Just because certain resorts are full of young people, doesn't mean you have to go there if this isn't your scene. Likewise, if it is – fill your boots and go for it!

Q. Help, I'm thinking of going on holiday parent-free for the first time

Firstly, it's natural to feel a bit nervous. For one, you are going to have to be responsible for things. If you are going abroad, you are going to need a passport and you are going to have to ensure you don't lose it.

You will also have to make sure that you look after all your money and other travel documents such as accommodation reservations and flight tickets. Many travel companies now supply tickets electronically to use via a mobile phone. If you have tickets stored this way, then you are going to have to make sure you don't lose your phone either. And make sure it's charged!

Staying in the UK makes things easier, but it's not going to be hot enough for you to spend two weeks on a beach getting a great tan. If it's guaranteed sun you want, then you need to go abroad.

Travelling abroad will invariably involve communicating in a foreign language. In most places you will find English is spoken, but if you make a effort to speak a little of the language it will usually be well received by the locals. However, you could equally be faced with the same issues if you have a strong local accent and travel around the UK. Though trying a local accent in the UK might not be as well received as trying some basic Spanish or Greek!

A beach holiday also has the advantage that whilst you are lying on it – you aren't really spending any money. Whether you are sleeping off the night before or simply recharging your batteries, laying on a towel is much cheaper than touring a city or entertaining yourself in the UK when it's raining.

Going on holiday parent-free for the first time is a fantastic experience whether you go to bed at 11pm or 6am. A holiday should simply be an extension of the things that you enjoy doing. There is no such thing as the perfect holiday – everyone is different and if you go somewhere that you want to go, it will be a memorable experience.

Q. Does it matter who you go with?

One of the first questions you will need to ask is who do you go with? If you are thinking about doing this as a 17/18 year old (or older) then it is likely that your friendship group is fairly defined.

The last thing you want to do is to take somebody away with you who isn't going to enjoy it. If they aren't enjoying it – then none of you will. You also need to bear in mind that you will be spending a lot of time in each other's company. Without doubt, a 'friend's holiday' will test the strength of your relationship. If one of you can be a bit moody, or has a bad habit that you can't really stand, it will rise to the top eventually. Holidays can be stressful, and if one of your party rocks the boat – everyone can end up getting wet.

Everyone thinks that their 'squad' will be different, but many people have returned from holiday with less friends than they went with. This could be for a number of reasons. They might "fall in love" and spend all their time with their new BF/GF, they might borrow your phone and lose it, or they simply might get so drunk one night that they tell everyone what they really feel about them. This can be exacerbated when you are all in one hot, sticky room and you still have seven days of your holiday to go. Picking your holiday friends is as important as picking your holiday location.

Q. Where should I go?

Package holiday or create your own?

As with everything, it starts with the question: "How much have you got to spend?"

Firstly, avoid the school summer holidays (July/August) as the prices are likely to be at their highest and it's when all the parents with children go away. The last thing you want is to go on a parent-free holiday and be faced with lots of other parents having a go at you because you are having too much fun.

Q. How much will it cost?

The three main costs of a holiday are:
- How much does it cost to travel there?
- How much does accommodation cost there?
- How much does it cost to live whilst you are there?

How much does it cost to travel there?

Most people take a holiday away from home, and this means you have to travel to get there.

If you have your own transport – the extra cost of going on holiday could merely be the extra amount of petrol required. If you already own a car, you could probably travel the entire length of the UK (from Land's End to John O'Groats – 837 miles) for around £160 worth of petrol. And don't forget – if there are four of you travelling, then its only £40/person.

If you don't have a car you might need to travel by coach or train. Traditionally the coach is cheaper, but if you book far enough ahead, you might find you can travel a long way from home for £150/person.

The big cost comes when you travel abroad. The fact that the UK is an island means that you need to travel over (or under) the sea to reach another country.

This means travelling by either a ferry, an aeroplane or via the Channel Tunnel. A ferry will get you to mainland Europe, but if you then want to travel further afield you are back to requiring a car (you can travel with your car on certain boats) or getting on a train or coach.

Most young adults travelling abroad do so by aeroplane. If you are looking to arrange your travel and accommodation separately (more later) you can book a return flight to a holiday destination (such as Greece) for as little as £200/person. Obviously, it will cost you a bit to get to and from the airport, but with a number of you travelling, these costs can be split and minimised. Planning ahead and booking flights as soon as they come out (9-12 months before you travel) will enable you to get the best deals.

DESTINATION ADULTHOOD | 205

How much does accommodation cost there?

For some holidays abroad you can book the travel and accommodation together. This is known as a 'package holiday' and they are run by holiday companies such as TUI, Thomas Cook and many more.

Most holidays are advertised online and they also exist in travel brochures that can be obtained from a travel agents. These holidays range in prices from £300/person through to as much as you want to pay. The amount varies depending on the type of holiday you want.

If you just want sun and somewhere to sleep, then for the first time in this book, you are going to be able to benefit from the lowest prices on offer! It has been said throughout this book that as a young adult it is important to set realistic expectations and booking a holiday is no exception. The more facilities you want, the more luxurious accommodation that you want, the better flight times that you want (during the day vs. flying in the middle of the night), the more the price is going to increase. But if you want a self-catering apartment - where you have to sort all your own meals - in a Greek resort in September, for a week, you should be able to get that for around £350/person.

Booking a package holiday also means that you have someone (a holiday rep) in the resort who will get you from the airport to your hotel (and will help you if anything goes wrong). They are also useful for giving you the inside knowledge for where to go – and where to avoid - in the local area.

It also means that you (and your parents) know where you are and - if you book through a reputable company – it comes with a certain level of reassurance that you don't necessarily have as an independent traveller. However, the growth of Airbnb and reviews on sites such as TripAdvisor mean that the risks associated with booking your own accommodation, and travelling independently, have been significantly minimised.

Of course, if you are more of an independent spirit you might want to sort your own accommodation. A quick Google search will show thousands of hotels, B&Bs, and hostels where you can stay – and often this can be a cheaper way of travelling. It also means that you don't have to stay in the same place for the whole holiday. Book a room somewhere for a couple of days and then move on to somewhere else.

Once you are in a location, you will usually be able to find lots of places to stay that aren't advertised online – however this method of sorting accommodation comes with a number of risks - will you find accommodation? Will it be safe? How much will it be? Many people travel this way and they embrace the freedom and the unpredictability that it brings.

How much does it cost to live whilst you are there?

Even though you are on holiday, you are still going to need to eat. How much you have to spend on a day to day basis will depend on the type of accommodation you book. Some holidays come with all the meals paid for, whilst some don't offer meals at all. You can tell what is provided by looking at what is known as the 'Board'.

These are the descriptions you will see in holiday listings:

- Room Only (As it says – just a bed – no food supplied and no kitchen to prepare anything
- Self Catering (Like 'Room Only' – but it will have a small kitchen area)
- Bed & Breakfast (breakfast provided but no other meal)
- Half Board (breakfast and evening meal provided)
- Full Board (breakfast, lunch and evening meal provided)
- All Inclusive (Full Board but with free drinks and snacks too)

Don't forget, that every meal provided is one that you have paid for as part of the total price of your holiday.

For most, having a parent-free holiday means late nights and lie-ins. Breakfast will be probably be served between around 6.30am and 10am. If you aren't planning on getting up till lunchtime, then paying for breakfast is a waste of money. Likewise, if you are happy enough just having a sandwich for lunch (brunch) and going to a cheap local restaurant for an evening meal – then you might save money by booking 'Room Only'. It's about booking the best (and most appropriate) holiday for you and your friends. Just because your parents like to get up at 8am to have breakfast doesn't mean that you have to.

However, when you start to eat independently, you can find that your money starts to disappear quickly. That sandwich for lunch can turn into a burger, chips and few beers whilst that evening meal soon adds up if you add wine and some starters.

One of the best ways to manage your holiday costs is to set yourself a daily budget. If you set yourself £50/day (and this is within your budget) you will know that buying a £20 inflatable crocodile means that you have only £30 left for the day and that's before eating or going out for the evening.

Finally if you are going to go abroad - you will also need to think about travel and health insurance (the latter is currently covered in Europe by applying for a free EHIC - European Health Insurance Card). You will also need to check brochures or online to see if you need any visas or whether there are any tourism taxes. Some countries are introducing one or both as a way of increasing border security and raising additional revenue. Simply type 'Visas required for [insert name of country]' or 'Tourist taxes for [insert name of country]' to find out if your holiday location is going to cost you any extra.

As a example the ESTA (which is the UK visa for the United States) costs around £70/person, whilst local tourism taxes for Spain cost around £20/person.

Q. What if I don't want to go abroad?

Whilst a holiday in the sun is great, borrowing a tent and camping in the middle of nowhere can be just as much fun, as can getting a group of you together to visit a friend that has moved away. There are lots of places that are brilliant to visit in the UK and there is definitely something for everyone - whether it be a mountain, the seaside or bustling cities.

Staying in the UK also helps reduce your carbon footprint too - so not only are you enriching your soul by being away from home, you are also saving the planet too.

Finally, don't underestimate the parent holiday. As much as going away with your friends is great, don't immediately turn your back on that family holiday. You might not get the freedom of going on holiday without them, but you can still have a great time without it costing you a fortune.

Why is the LifeLocation® Travelling important?

Travelling and visiting somewhere different rarely lets you down. Even if it doesn't meet your expectations you invariable gain a new set of shared memories that you will recount with friends for the whole of your life.

There are so many places to visit and so many different ways to discover them, that it is easy to find a number of ideal places that will enrich your soul and fuel your passions.

And it doesn't have a cost a lot of money. There are travel options available for every budget so go out there and explore!

Further Links

www.destination.org.uk - *Lots of specially commissioned and curated content relating to travelling*

Search **local authority websites** for lists of local travelling information

Pitch Up Campsites
www.pitchup.com

Youth Hostels
www.yha.org.uk

Foreign Travel Advice
www.gov.uk/foreign-travel-advice

STA
www.statravel.co.uk/tours-worldwide.htm

Student Universe
www.studentuniverse.co.uk/tours

Trip Adviser
www.tripadvisor.co.uk

Real gap experience
www.realgap.co.uk

Interrailing
www.interrail.eu/en

Camp America
www.campamerica.co.uk

National Express
www.nationalexpress.com

Resetting your travelling and holiday options

Soft and Factory Resets

- **Worried about going away on your own?** Why not spend a night away somewhere close to home and slowly build up to a longer break away?

This All Sounds Too Much. My Destination Adulthood Is To Just Become A Rich, Famous Celebrity!

The journey to becoming an adult is hard work and expensive. Why go through all the effort of getting an education or a good paying job when you can just become famous and earn loads?

In fairness, if you can pull it off it's a great strategy. Appear on a reality show, be loved/hated by the public, get a million social media followers and 'boom' you've done it. Get 'papped' in Barbados on a jet ski and be paid a fortune to promote the latest hair and beauty products.

The first thing to ask is 'Do you want to be rich or do you want to be famous?'

This might seem like a daft question as surely the two go hand in hand? However, it is very easy to become a famous celebrity without being rich. Just because someone is at an event wearing an expensive outfit or item of jewellery doesn't mean it belongs to them. Likewise, seeing an Instagram post of someone driving an expensive car doesn't mean it's theirs.

Projecting an image of being famous and rich is different to being famous and rich. Most proper A-list (movie and music) stars are rarely seen unless they are promoting something. However, open a newspaper or gossip magazine and it is the same 50 people who have gained weight, lost weight, got married, got divorced or done something they shouldn't have. For them, being famous is their job and their job is to help sell magazines, newspapers and advertise products. And this is a tough 16-hours/day job that starts on Breakfast TV, and finishes when their publicist has arranged with the photographer for them to leave a nightclub at 3am.

So how do you become a celebrity? Well firstly you are going to have to work hard, really hard. Never forget that this is a job.

Having a job means that you give something (your time and effort) in exchange for something (a wage, profile, experience, or an opportunity). We discussed in Employment that when large numbers of people can do a job (or want to do a job), the wage that an employer has to pay is lower. So, with lots of people keen to be famous, the pay is going to be low at the beginning of your celebrity status - and it will be a while till you are buying that jet-ski!

Q. How can I become famous?

There are lots to routes to becoming famous, but for the purposes here we will look at three:
- Becoming a 'YouTube sensation',
- Appearing on a reality TV show / talent show or
- Doing it naturally

Becoming a YouTube sensation

If you have a phone with a camera – you can make a vlog. Once you've made one, you can set up a YouTube account for free and upload it. 'Boom' done. Tell your mates, get them to promote in on their social media feeds and watch those views and subscriptions accelerate upwards - 'Double Boom'. Now you're a famous vlogger and everyone will send you free stuff and pay you loads of money – 'Triple Boom'!

Except they won't. YouTube say that there are over 25,000 channels that have over 100,000 subscribers (and this was in 2016), so the market is pretty crowded. If you want to stand out you are going to have to offer something that 25,000 other people aren't already doing (or if they are – do the same thing but differently or better). With over 1.3bn channels on YouTube there are significantly more that don't have large subscribers than do.

So the big question is: "what are you vlogging about and why should people give up their own time to watch you?"

Firstly you are going to have to constantly update your channel with new content which means that you are going to have to regularly vlog and keep your subscribers engaged. Uploading one vlog a week will probably take you two days to plan and film (10 hours) which means that is either your weekend gone or your weekday evenings. If this is starting to sound like a job – that is because that's exactly what it is. Except at the start you aren't being paid.

This means that your vlogging topic has to be something that you are really interested in. The last thing you want, is to be famous and successful in something that you aren't that bothered about. Also, you will find in the early stages that the 'perks' that you receive will be related to what you Vlog about. This will either be 'directly' (i.e. beauty products if you run a beauty blog) or products that potential companies believe your subscriber audience would be interested in.

So vlogging might make you famous, but it isn't going to immediately make you rich. You will only make money from your vlog depending on who the people are that are watching it – and what advertisers can sell to them. If your audience is 10-year-old girls then beyond Claire's Accessories, Lush and hair bows, your market might be limited, but if your audience is 18-25 year-old males (and you have a large number of subscribers) – then advertisers will be queuing up for you to talk about their products.

The key thing to take away from this is that you are going to have to do a lot of work building your channel before you will become either rich or famous or if you are lucky, both.

Prior to the 'social media influencer' explosion, most people only did it because they were interested in vlogging about a subject they had a passion about. Those that stuck at it then got their rewards as their popularity increased. For many people considering this route they will find that the boat has already sailed, and that nobody wants another beauty blog. The next batch of successful people will be those that get on board the next big thing – whatever that is.

Appearing on a reality TV show or talent show

Do you have a talent?' Can you sing, dance or generally entertain people? If you can then why not consider appearing on a talent show?

In reality, if you can do these things you have probably been part of either a club or group where you have had chance to showcase your skills. If you were really good enough, someone (excluding family members) would have told you and encouraged you to do something with your talent. Most theatre and dance groups are inundated by production companies asking people to audition for shows. If you haven't been put forward, then you have to ask why not?

Without being too cynical or revealing the secrets, the audition stages of TV talent shows are largely exercises to promote the forthcoming show. Aspiring performers undertake multiple auditions before they are anywhere near the celebrity judges. But the real secret is that most of the people you see on TV auditioning have been fast-tracked from theatre and performance drama schools and not the many thousands you saw queuing up outside the various arenas around the country.

Getting selected for a show is only the start. If a major organisation is going to invest in you to be their star, they need to ensure that you are going to be able to do the job. The multiple-episode TV show process is designed for a number of reasons: 1) it allows the public to see if they like you, but most importantly 2) it allows the production staff to monitor your work ethic and decide whether you are cut out for the job.

What they are really auditioning you on is 'will you work hard?', 'Do you get on with people?', 'Do you get mood swings?', 'How will you handle 'fame'?', but most importantly – 'can you be relied on to deliver?'. So, when negative stories appear about a contestant (that subsequently loses them some popularity), or when judges vote someone out (who everyone thought was going to win) – it's just the way the game is played to ensure that the person who is most equipped for the hard work wins. Obviously not all TV shows work like this – but quite a few do.

And this is a theme that will continue once you are famous. If you fail to deliver what is required from you, there will always be a pool of young people ready to take your place.

The same goes for people applying for TV reality shows. TV production staff are very good at knowing what makes a good reality star. This is their job and they are paid very well to make the correct decisions.

Just because you appear on a show doesn't mean that

you will automatically become rich and famous. Again, it will be a combination of how you appear on screen and how you behave off screen. There are thousands of people that could look good on screen and be liked by the general public, but how many of them would be liked by a production manager who might need to spend lots of time in their company.

Specific reality TV shows might demand a cocky, arrogant personality but it needs to be switch on & off-able, as no one wants to spend time with someone like that off screen. The 'cocky and arrogant personality' is just one element of your job – the other elements are the same as any other job – turn up on time, be polite to your co-workers and do what is it expected from you. And if you don't work hard and deliver this – then your fame game will be over. Just. like. that.

Doing it naturally

The third way is to let it happen naturally. For most people, becoming rich and/or famous was a bi-product of doing something they loved doing. Authors, musicians, presenters, YouTubers, Instagram influencers all started because they had an interest in something. Yes, sure people want to be successful when they start out, but this is rarely the reason they do it.

Having a passion for something and then finding that you can earn money from it is one of the best feelings ever. Yes, you might play the guitar and dream of playing Wembley

Stadium, but most people are quite happy playing to a group of people in their local pub. Few people map the journey from bedroom or kitchen table to Wembley or an Oscar's party and then successfully executes it. Everyone's journey involves luck (both good and bad) and a host of barriers that you will need to find ways of overcoming.

These barriers allow you to get better at your chosen passion. They don't always feel like it at the time, but each time you overcome a problem you are better equipped to deal with the next one. Barriers will come in various shapes and sizes – family issues, additional commitments, making contacts and the constant need to improve and learn new ways of doing things. And then, even when you've done all of this you will be completely in the hands of luck. Some people never get the opportunity to showcase their abilities whilst some with less talent do. It is all about being in the right place at the right time. You put all the hard miles in and then you wait for your chance. And if it comes you need to make sure you take it.

Resetting your plan to become a rich, famous celebrity

Soft and Factory Resets

- **Thinking about starting a vlog but don't know how?**
  Use the camera on your phone and have a go. Look online for tips and the more videos you make, the more professional-looking they will become.
- **Is your blog not taking off?** Don't be surprised by this as it is really difficult to build a profile with a large number of followers. You could take an online marketing course or read one of the many guides online designed to increase followers.
- **Low audiences?** This is often quite relative - 1,000 to one person might seem low, but to others its really high. You might want to consider that even a small number of followers will still sound impressive in a job interview - especially if you can demonstrate how the skills you have used in building your audience can be transferred to the workplace.
- **Got a talent but it hasn't been recognised?**
  Why not create a network of people that might be able to help you realise your dream. Search online for professional representation and let them give you an impartial opinion of your chances of making it

Part Four: Reset, Plan, Take Responsibility & Make It Happen

So, there we have it, a helpful guide to reaching your Destination Adulthood.

If you have followed the steps and recommendations within the book you should have reached this point with a plan of what your Destination Adulthood is starting to look like and what you need to do to reach it.

Remember, your destination is unique to you and as much as everyone's Destination Adulthood will be different, so will the position you start from.

This book has been written for everyone who is about to start their journey, is midway through or is about to complete it. Rich or poor, educated or uneducated, qualified or unqualified, employed or unemployed, home owners or homeless. Everyone is different but where we are currently only defines the journey we have undertaken to date. It does not define our future journey.

The Reset

This is why we start by considering a reset. These are the basic things that we all need to sort before we can maximise our potential and effectively reach our desired destination. For some it will be a soft reset – a minor change in our daily routine that makes a small but important difference to how we proceed in life. But for others, some changes might necessitate a full-on factory reset – a change that cannot be undertaken overnight. A change that will require support from others, a commitment to follow through and an almost certain requirement to push yourself out of your comfort zone.

All resets are relative. What one person considers difficult is easy for someone else. We all have our strengths and we are happy to make them stronger. Unfortunately we are less happy to confront our weaknesses and it is often easier to simply ignore them. However, failing to address them lets them fester, which means they start to beat us and stop us from being the person that we want to be and living the life we want to live.

Did you write a list of the areas that you need to reset? It will provide you with a list of the barriers that you are going to need to overcome in order to reach your Destination Adulthood. Remember if you want to keep them private, why not jot them down in your notes on your mobile phone?

Areas that need a reset	How am I going to reset them?

The Plan

Did you make a note of your potential Destination Adulthood in the introduction? Did you do this before you had read the rest of the book? Is it still relevant or have your thoughts changed?

As this is your plan, you can change it whenever you want. We all change our minds as we get older and you will be no exception. It's the reason we change our jobs, move house, visit different places. People evolve and you will too.

What your destination looks like at 18 will be different to what it is at 25. The key is when you choose to start planning. If you start planning at 18, then your plan as a 25 year old will be a continuation of the 18 year old version of yourself. The only difference is that it will be refined, developed and be a better suited plan based on the experiences and the journey you are travelling on. If you don't have a plan you will find that the destination you are travelling towards as a 25 year old is undefined and has been left to chance. For some it will work out fine, but for others it will lead to a dead-end that you feel you can't reverse out of.

Each of the chapters and LifeLocations® in this book should have given you plenty of options to think about in terms of how you want your adult life to pan out. You should now have an idea of how much money you are going to need to keep yourself warm, clothed and entertained and what this means in terms of employment, education and skills development. Now is the time to think about the difficult questions and deal with the even harder answers.

Everyone's Destination Adulthood is unique. It will not be exactly the same as your best friends and as a result you will have a different journey to reach it. This is not to say that you can't share some or most of the elements but it is important that you remember why you are making your choices You are doing them for the benefit of you and not necessarily your friend.

If you want a lifestyle based on money, then you are going to need a plan to ensure that it happens. If you want a job based on something you feel passionate about then you need to ensure that you have the correct qualifications and the right networks to maximise your chances of achieving it. It is never too early to start planning.

What does my Destination Adulthood look like?	What do I need to do in order to make it happen?

Take Responsibility

There is only one person who is going to be responsible for ensuring you get to your unique Destination Adulthood – and that's YOU. Sure, lots of people will be able to help you, but you will be the one that needs to take advantage of the opportunities when they are presented or seek them out when they aren't.

This is obviously hard for some people, but that is even more reason to take responsibility for your own actions. Perhaps the reason it is hard is because you need to increase some of your employability skills? In which case you need to take responsibility for this and perhaps volunteer somewhere locally? It is simply too easy to blame someone else for not maximising your potential.

Lots of things will have happened that have resulted in where you are right now, but remember, they are in the past. How things turn out in the future is up to you and by taking responsibility for your own actions now, you can best ensure that you reach your Destination Adulthood.

Make it happen

Every single one of us is a superhero. We have a range of powers that can enable us to do super human things – things that many of us don't know we can. In order to harness these powers, they need to be developed, tested and used on a regular basis.

We all have the power to stop and look at our lives and change some of the things that aren't working as well as they should be. When we put our minds to it, we can adapt to changing situations and we can overcome problems. When we do this, and when we look back at what we have achieved it never ceases to amaze us.

We have the ability to look into the future and see what it holds for us. This allows us to decide if this is what we want our future to be. If it isn't we have the power to change it. It might take all our strength and reserves, but we have the ability to shift the direction that our life is travelling in. Yes, it might occasionally mean one step backwards, but when we start to go forward again, we will be doing it quicker and more purposefully than we were before.

When we set our mind to a task we can make it happen. So, reset if necessary, plan your journey, take responsibility for your actions and make your Destination Adulthood a reality.

I'll look forward to seeing you there!